Contents

IVY MANNING

Servings: 10

INGREDIENTS

- 1/4 cup all purpose flour
- 2 pounds paneer or firm or extra-firm tofu, cut into 3/4- to 1-inch cubes
- 2 large onions, cut into 1- to 2-inch pieces
- 2 teaspoons cumin seeds
- 2/3 cup usli ghee, divided
- 1/4 cup minced peeled fresh ginger
- 6 garlic cloves, minced
- 1 1/2 tablespoons ground coriander
- 2 serrano chile, minced with seeds
- 2 ounces 28- can crushed tomatoes with added purée
- 1 cup water
- 2 teaspoons turmeric
- 3 cups shelled fresh peas (from about 1 1/2 pounds peas in pods) or 1 1/2 cups frozen peas, thawed
- 2 teaspoons garam masala
- 2/3 cup chopped fresh cilantro
- steamed basmati rice
- paneer, a fresh cow's milk or buffalo's-milk cheese, and usli ghee (clarified butter; also called ghee) are sold at some natural foods stores and at indian markets. if you can't find paneer, then tofu, chicken, shrimp, or scallops would also work well in this recipe. clarified butter or vegetable oil can be used in place of the ghee.
- garam masala is a curry spice blend that's available in the spice section of many supermarkets, at indian markets, and from thespicehouse.com.

DIRECTIONS

1. Place flour in a moderate bowl. Add paneer to bowl; toss to coating with flour. Heat 2 tablespoons ghee in a weighty large nonstick skillet over medium-high heat. Shake excessive flour from paneer; increase skillet and make until browned in places, turning occasionally, about 4 mins. Transfer paneer to plate; reserve. Reserve skillet.

2. Place onion items in the processor chip. Using on/off turns, procedure until finely chopped however, not watery. Temperature staying 3 tablespoons ghee in reserved skillet over moderate temperature. Add cumin seeds and mix until aromatic, about 1 minute. Add cut onion and make until starting to brown, stirring frequently, about ten minutes. Add minced ginger, minced garlic, floor coriander, and minced serrano chile with seeds; mix 1 minute. Add crushed tomatoes with puree, 1/2 cup drinking water, and

turmeric; provide to simmer. Reduce temperature to moderate low; cover and simmer until blend thickens somewhat and flavors mix, stirring occasionally, about quarter-hour.

3. Add shelled refreshing peas and prepared paneer; lightly fold to include evenly. Cook mixture more than medium-low temperature until peas are tender and paneer can be heated through, folding occasionally about five minutes. Fold in garam masala and cilantro. Time of year curry to flavor with salt and pepper. Serve with steamed basmati rice.

MARIA HELM SINSKEY

Servings: 10

INGREDIENTS

- 2 cups plain whole-milk yogurt
- 1/2 cup coarsely chopped fresh cilantro
- 2 tablespoons garam masala
- 1 1/2 tablespoons coarse kosher salt
- 6 tablespoons extra-virgin olive oil
- 2 large garlic cloves, pressed
- 2 - to 4 1/2-pound roasting chicken, cut into 8 pieces, backbone removed
- 4 small onions, cut into 1/4-inch-thick slices

DIRECTIONS

1. Combine yogurt, chopped cilantro, essential olive oil, garam masala, salt, and garlic in a 13x9x2-inch cup baking dish. Add poultry to marinade, 1 piece at the same time, covering all sides. Cover with plastic material wrap; refrigerate for at least 2 hours. Perform AHEAD Could be made one day ahead. Keep refrigerated.

2. Position racks in the best third and bottom level third of oven; preheat to 400°F. Arrange onions in thin level on a large rimmed baking sheet to create a bed for the chicken. Best with chicken parts in a single level, spacing apart for also roasting (chicken it's still covered with marinade). Discard staying marinade.

3. Roast chicken at the top rack until prepared through and juices run very clear when the thickest part of the thigh is certainly pierced with a knife, about one hour. Serve poultry atop onion slices. Spoon pan juices around.

DAWN PERRY

Servings: 10

INGREDIENTS

- 1/2 cup (1/2 stick) unsalted butter, room temperature

- 2 teaspoons kosher salt
- 1 teaspoon ground turmeric
- 1 teaspoon ground coriander
- 2 teaspoons ground cumin
- 1 teaspoon freshly ground black pepper
- 1 teaspoon ground cinnamon
- 1/2 teaspoon ground cardamom

DIRECTIONS

1. Process all substances in a food processor chip until smooth.
2. DO AHEAD: Butter could be made 5 times ahead. Wrap firmly and chill, or freeze up to at least one 1 month.

MARK THOMAS

Servings: 10

INGREDIENTS

- nonstick vegetable oil spray
- 3 cups all purpose flour
- 1/2 teaspoon salt
- 1 1/2 cups (1 1/2 sticks) unsalted butter, room temperature
- 2 teaspoons ground ginger
- 1/2 cup sugar
- 2 large egg yolk
- 1/2 cup minced crystallized ginger
- 8 (8-ounce) packages cream cheese, room temperature
- 2 1/2 cups sugar
- 2 (8-ounce) containers mascarpone cheese (italian cream cheese)
- 10 large eggs
- 4 large eggs yolks
- 1 1/2 tablespoons ground ginger
- 1 1/2 tablespoons ground cardamom
- 1 teaspoon vanilla extract
- 1/2 teaspoon ground allspice
- 1/2 teaspoon salt
- 1/4 teaspoon ground black pepper
- 2 2/3 cups sour cream

- 6 tablespoons sugar
- 1 1/2 tablespoons vanilla extract

DIRECTIONS

1. Spray a 9-inch-size springform pan with 3-inch-high sides with nonstick spray. Sift flour, ginger, and salt into a moderate bowl. Using an electrical mixer, defeat butter and sugar in another moderate bowl until blended. Defeat in egg yolk, after that flour mixture. Mix in crystallized ginger. Collect dough into ball; flatten into a disk. Roll from floured surface to 9-in. round. Transfer to ready pan. Press onto the bottom level and 1 in. up sides of pan; pierce around with a fork. Freeze thirty minutes.

2. Position rack in the middle of the oven and preheat to 350°F. Line crust with foil; fill up with dried coffee beans or pie weights. Bake until established, about thirty minutes. Remove foil and coffee beans. Bake crust until golden dark brown and cooked through, about 20 minutes. Great crust totally on the rack.

3. Preheat oven to 350°F. Using an electric mixer, defeat cream cheese and sugar in a large bowl until smooth, about three minutes. Add mascarpone; defeat until smooth. Beat entirely eggs, 1 at the same time, then defeat in yolks. Add following 6 ingredients; defeat until blended. Transfer filling to cooled crust in pan; smooth top.

4. Bake cake for one hour. Reduce oven heat range to 200°F. Continue baking until cake is defined around edges but center moves somewhat when the pan is carefully shaken (best of the cake may crack), about thirty minutes longer.

5. Remove cake from the oven. Increase oven heat range to 350°F.

6. Whisk all substances in normal size bowl; spread equally over the best of the cake. Bake until established, about ten minutes. Run a little knife around cake sides. Chill uncovered over night. DO AHEAD Could be produced 2 days forward. Chill until cold, after that cover and maintain chilled.

7. Remove pan sides. Transfer cake to a platter. Cut into wedges and provide.

MASALA DOSA

Servings: 5

INGREDIENTS

- 1/2 pound . russet potatoes (about 1 large potato)
- 1/2 teaspoon black mustard seeds
- 1/2 tbsp. chana dal, also known as split yellow gram lentils or split husked black or brown chickpeas
- 1 tbsp. ghee (clarified butter) or olive oil, plus more for brushing or drizzling
- 1/2 tbsp. urad dal, also known as split husked black gram lentils, or ivory white lentils (they are white in color)
- 1/2 large yellow onion (8 oz.), halved and thinly sliced
- 1/2 large jalapeño or 2 medium serrano chiles, diced (1/4 cup)

- 3/8 teaspoon kosher salt, plus more to taste
- pinch of ground turmeric
- 1 tbsp. coarsely chopped fresh cilantro leaves
- 1 teaspoon 2-3 fresh lemon juice
- 1/4 cup packaged spiced chutney powder (also known as pudi or masala chutney powder)
- 2 tablespoons ghee (clarified butter) or olive oil

DIRECTIONS

1. Prepare the potato sabzi: Fill a medium pot about two-thirds of precisely how with water. Bring to a boil and add the potato; allow make until potato feels merely tender every time a paring knife is normally inserted into the center, about 25 occasions. Remove and let amazing slightly, from then on peel and break into bite-size pieces.

2. In a pan set over moderate heat, add both 2 tablespoons ghee or oil. Once warm, add the mustard seeds and make, providing the pan a great shake every handful of mere seconds, before seeds pop and sputter, about 2 minutes. Lower temperature to medium-low and add the chana dal and urad dal. Make, stirring sometimes, before dal is normally fragrant and lightly golden, 2-3 occasions. Add the onions and chiles and make, stirring sometimes, before onions are tender and translucent, 6-8 occasions. Add the potatoes, 3/4 teaspoon kosher salt, and the turmeric and blend well; prepare before potatoes have absorbed the spices and switched a pale yellowish, 8-10 occasions. (If the potatoes desire pasty and dry out, add normal water, mashing in 1 tablespoon simultaneously until they accomplish a lumpy but pliable consistency.) Taste and change the salt as desired.

3. Get rid of the filling from temperature and blend in the cilantro. Add the lemon juice to taste. Transfer to a bowl, cover, and reserve or refrigerate until you'll be prepared to cook the dosas.

4. Meanwhile, in just a little bowl, mix the gunpowder paste: Add the chutney powder and ghee or gas. Blend until easy paste forms, after that reserve. (Gunpowder paste can keep for a few weeks in the refrigerator.)

5. Heat a 12-inch nonstick pan or well-seasoned cast-iron griddle over medium-high temperature, or collect a nonstick electric griddle to medium-high. (If using cast iron, grease the very best lightly with gas.) Sprinkle a few drops of normal water on the popular surface area: It really is ready when the drops of normal water sizzle and evaporate instantly. Be sure the dosa batter is obviously well-stirred and clear of lumps, then ladle 1/3 cup of batter into the middle of the griddle. Functioning quickly but equally, and using underneath of the ladle, type the dosa by creating a continuous spiral motion, beginning in the guts and dragging the batter outward toward the pan's edges to make a large, linked bull's-eye form 10 in . in size. (If chosen, you can trickle and drag a lot more batter around the edges to fill the pan, and patch any too-slender areas or little holes with extra batter.) When the very best develops bubbles and looks merely place, quickly brush or drizzle simply a little ghee or oil (about 1 teaspoon) over the most effective as the dosa cooks, acquiring treatment to saturate the outer areas. When underneath is normally carefully crispy and golden darkish, about 5 minutes, you can fill the dosa, or utilize a spatula to flip the

dosa and sharpened all of those other sides if desired. (That's useful if you're not really used to dosa making and want to be sure thicker spots are properly ready through.) If flipping, drizzle just one more teaspoon of gas around the edges after flipping and make the various other aspects before thicker ridges of batter are set up but however versatile, 30-60 secs. Flip the dosa once more to make sure that the crispier, browner factor is on underneath. Spread 1 tablespoon of the gunpowder filling over the lighter surface of the dosa.

6. Fill up the dosa in the pan if desired: Spoon 1/4 cup of the potato sabzi onto the guts of the dosa in its lighter factor, using the trunk of the spoon to spread and press the filling into a thin layer to make sure that it heats evenly. Correctly loosen the perimeter of the dosa with an established spatula, from then on slide the spatula beneath the middle to dislodge. Make use of the spatula to coax one benefit of the dosa softly to the various other aspects, tucking the advantage relatively within the crêpe to produce a high cylindrical roll. Additionally, you can fold the dosa into thirds like a letter.

7. Remove to a plate and serve immediately with coconut chutney and further gunpower paste and potato sabzi if desired. Eat using your hands.

8. Prepare the potato sabzi: Fill a medium pot about two-thirds of precisely how with water. Bring to a boil and add the potato; allow make until potato feels basically tender every time a paring knife is obviously inserted into the center, about 25 a couple of minutes. Remove and allow great slightly, from then on peel and break into bite-size pieces.

9. In a pan set over moderate heat, add both 2 tablespoons ghee or oil. Once scorching, add the mustard seeds and make, offering the pan a great shake every handful of mere seconds, before seeds pop and sputter, about 2 minutes. Lower warmth to medium-low and add the chana dal and urad dal. Make, stirring sometimes, before dal is obviously fragrant and softly golden, 2-3 a couple of minutes. Add the onions and chiles and make, stirring sometimes, before onions are tender and translucent, 6-8 a couple of minutes. Add the potatoes, 3/4 teaspoon kosher salt, and the turmeric and blend well; prepare before potatoes have absorbed the spices and switched a pale yellowish, 8-10 a couple of minutes. (If the potatoes desire pasty and dry out, add normal water, mashing in 1 tablespoon simultaneously until they get yourself a lumpy but pliable consistency.) Taste and adapt the salt as recommended.

10. Get rid of the filling from temperature and combine in the cilantro. Add the lemon juice to taste. Transfer to a bowl, cover, and reserve or refrigerate until you'll be prepared to cook the dosas.

11. Meanwhile, in just a little bowl, combine the gunpowder paste: Add the chutney powder and ghee or gas. Mix until straightforward paste forms, after that reserve. (Gunpowder paste can keep for a few weeks in the refrigerator.)

12. Heat a 12-inch nonstick pan or well-seasoned cast-iron griddle over medium-high temperature, or collect a nonstick electric griddle to medium-high. (If using cast iron, grease the very best lightly with gas.) Sprinkle a few drops of normal water on the popular surface area: It really is ready when the drops of normal water sizzle and evaporate instantly. Be sure the dosa batter is certainly well-stirred and clear of lumps, then ladle 1/3 cup of batter into the middle of the griddle. Functioning quickly but equally, and

using underneath of the ladle, type the dosa by creating a continuous spiral motion, beginning in the guts and dragging the batter outward toward the pan's edges to make a large, linked bull's-eye form 10 ins in size. (If favored, you can trickle and drag a lot more batter around the edges to fill the pan, and patch any too-thin areas or little holes with extra batter.) When the very best develops bubbles and looks just place, quickly brush or drizzle simply a little ghee or oil (about 1 teaspoon) over the most effective as the dosa cooks, acquiring treatment to saturate the outer areas. When underneath is usually softly crispy and golden darkish, about 5 minutes, you can fill the dosa, or utilize a spatula to flip the dosa and sharpened all of those other sides if desired. (That's useful if you're not really used to dosa making and want to be sure thicker spots are properly ready through.) If flipping, drizzle just one more teaspoon of gas around the edges after flipping and make the various other aspects before thicker ridges of batter are set up but nevertheless flexible, 30-60 a few moments. Flip the dosa once more to make sure that the crispier, browner component is on underneath. Spread 1 tablespoon of the gunpowder filling over the lighter surface of the dosa.

13. Fill the dosa about the pan if desired: Spoon 1/4 cup of the potato sabzi onto the guts of the dosa about its lighter component, using the trunk of the spoon to spread and press the filling into a thin layer to make sure that it heats equally. Cautiously loosen the perimeter of the dosa with an arranged spatula, from then on slide the spatula beneath the middle to dislodge. Make use of the spatula to coax one benefit of the dosa softly to the additional part, tucking the advantage relatively within the crêpe to create a high cylindrical roll. However, you can fold the dosa into thirds like a letter.

14. Remove to a plate and serve immediately with coconut chutney and further gunpower paste and potato sabzi if desired. Eat using your hands.

CUCUMBER RAITA WITH BLACK MUSTARD AND CILANTRO

Servings: 10

INGREDIENTS

- 1 teaspoon cumin seeds
- 2 tablespoons sunflower or other neutral oils
- 6 persian cucumbers
- 6 cups plain whole-milk greek yogurt
- 2 teaspoons black or brown mustard seeds
- 2 tablespoons fresh lemon juice
- 2 garlic cloves, finely grated
- 2/3 cup finely chopped cilantro, plus sprigs for serving
- kosher salt

- kashmiri chili powder or paprika (for serving)

DIRECTIONS

1. Toast cumin seeds in a dried-out small saucepan over moderate heat, shaking pan frequently, until fragrant, about 45 secs. Transfer to a plate and allow great. Coarsely grind in a spice mill or coarsely chop with a chef's knife; reserve for serving.

2. Temperature oil and mustard seeds in a little skillet over moderate until seeds start to pop, about 1 minute. Let great.

3. Grate cucumbers in the moderate holes of a box grater; squeeze out surplus liquid together with your hands and transfer to a moderate bowl. Combine in yogurt, lemon juice, garlic, and ⅓ glass cilantro; period with salt.

4. To serve, drizzle raita with mustard essential oil, sprinkle with chili powder and reserved cumin, and best with cilantro sprigs.

MATT DUCKOR

Servings: 10

INGREDIENTS

- 1/4 cup red wine vinegar
- 1/4 cup tandoori paste
- 8 garlic cloves, minced
- 2 medium head of cauliflower (about 1 1/2 pound), cut into bite-size florets (about 4 cups)
- 2 cups cornstarch
- kosher salt
- tandoori masala (optional)
- a deep-fry thermometer

DIRECTIONS

1. Whisk garlic, vinegar, tandoori paste, and 2 tablespoons of oil in a sizable bowl to mix. Add cauliflower and toss to totally layer florets. Marinate at area heat range for at least one hour, or cover and chill overnight.

2. Attach deep-fry thermometer aside of a big large pot. Pour in essential oil to a depth of just one 1 inch. Heat essential oil over medium-high temperature to 350°.

3. Place cornstarch in a moderate bowl. Dealing with a few florets at the same time, toss cauliflower in cornstarch, after transfer to a coarse-mesh sieve, shaking unwanted cornstarch back to the bowl. Place florets on a rimmed baking sheet.

4. Employed in batches, fry florets till light golden and crispy, 3-4 a few minutes per batch. Transfer to a paper towel-lined plate to drain. Period with salt and dirt with tandoori masala, if preferred.

METHI MALAI PANEER (CREAMY FENUGREEK AND SPINACH WITH CHEESE)

Servings: 8

INGREDIENTS

- 4 tbsp. canola oil
- 1/2 cup cashews
- 1/4 cup garlic, minced
- 1 small red onion, minced
- 1 teaspoon cumin seeds
- 1 pound baby spinach
- 2/3 pound fenugreek, trimmed and roughly chopped, or 4 cups frozen chopped fenugreek, defrosted
- 1/2 pound paneer, coarsely grated
- 1 cup frozen peas
- 1/2 cup heavy cream
- 4 tbsp. unsalted butter
- 1 teaspoon red chile powder, such as cayenne
- 1 teaspoon garam masala
- 1 teaspoon ground coriander
- 1 teaspoon ground cumin
- 1 teaspoon ground turmeric
- 6 canned whole, peeled tomatoes, drained and crushed by hand
- kosher salt, to taste
- naan, for serving (optional)

DIRECTIONS

1. Warmth oil in a 12" skillet over medium-high. Make cashews and cumin seeds until fragrant and seeds start to pop, 1-2 moments. Add garlic and onion; cook until golden, 3-4 moments. Add spinach and fenugreek; cook until wilted, 2-3 moments. Add paneer, peas, cream, butter, cayenne, garam masala, coriander, cumin, turmeric, tomatoes, salt, and 1/4 cup drinking water; boil. Reduce warmth to medium; make, covered, and stirring sometimes, until mixture is somewhat thickened about 25 moments. Serve with naan, if you want.

DAIKON CURRY

Servings: 8

INGREDIENTS

- 4 tbsp. canola oil
- 1 teaspoon ajwain (carom) seeds
- 1/4 cup garlic, minced
- 2 pounds . daikon with greens, peeled and cut into 1/2" pieces, greens trimmed and roughly chopped
- 1 teaspoon ground coriander
- 1 medium yellow onion, roughly chopped
- 1 teaspoon ground cumin
- 1 teaspoon ground turmeric
- 1/2 teaspoon red chile powder, such as cayenne
- 2 teaspoons amchur (green mango) powder
- kosher salt, to taste
- chapatis, for serving (optional)

DIRECTIONS

1. Warmth oil in a 12" skillet over medium-high high temperature. Make carom seeds until they pop, 1-2 a few minutes. Add garlic and onion; cook until golden, 5-7 minutes. Mix in daikon and its own leaves, the coriander, cumin, turmeric, and chile powder. Reduce high temperature to medium-low; make, covered, and stirring sometimes, until daikon is certainly tender about 20 minutes. Mix in amchur and salt; serve with chapatis, if you want.

RAJASTHANI WHITE CHICKEN CURRY

Servings: 8

INGREDIENTS

- 1/2 cup desiccated coconut
- 2 tbsp. white poppy seeds
- 50 whole white peppercorns
- 40 cashews
- 1 1/2 tablespoons pumpkins seeds
- 20 green cardamom pods
- 1 cup ghee
- 2 teaspoons kala jeera (black cumin)
- 12 whole cloves
- 8 black cardamom pods, cracked
- 4 indian or regular bay leaves

- 1 cup cinnamon
- 8 small green thai chiles or 2 serranos, halved
- 6 tablespoons garlic, minced
- 2 medium yellow onions, minced
- 2 pieces 1 (2") ginger, peeled and minced
- 2 (2 1/2–3-lb.) chicken, cut into 8 pieces, skin removed
- 1 1/2 cups plain, full-fat yogurt
- 1 1/2 whole milk
- 1 teaspoon ground mace
- kosher salt, to taste
- 4 tbsp. roughly chopped cilantro, for garnish

DIRECTIONS

1. Grind coconut, poppy seeds, pumpkin seeds, 15 white peppercorns, 10 cashews, and the green cardamom in a spice grinder right into a powder; set aside.
2. Melt ghee in a 6-qt. saucepan over medium-high heat. Make staying peppercorns, the Kala jeera, cloves, dark cardamom, bay leaves, and cinnamon until fragrant and seeds start to pop, 1-2 mins. Add chiles, garlic, onion, and ginger; prepare until golden, 8-10 mins. Add chicken, yogurt, milk, mace, and salt; boil. Reduce heat to moderate and mix in reserved spice powder; make, covered somewhat, and stirring sometimes, until chicken is prepared through, 20-22 mins. Using tongs, transfer chicken to a serving platter. Mix staying cashews into sauce; simmer until somewhat thickened, 4-6 a few minutes; spoon over chicken and garnish with cilantro.

CREAMY CASHEW INDIAN BUTTER PANEER...WITH FRIED PANEER!

Servings: 12

INGREDIENTS

- 1/4 cup coconut oil or ghee or butter
- 2 (14-ounce) cans coconut milk lite or regular
- 1 1/2 cups roasted cashews
- 1 pound paneer cheese cubed
- 2 (6 ounce) tomato paste can
- 1/2 cup greek yogurt or 1/4 cup more coconut milk for vegans
- 1 a small sweet onion diced
- 1/4 cup garlic minced or grated
- 2 tablespoons fresh ginger grated

- 1 1/2 tablespoons spicy curry powder
- 2 teaspoons 1-2 thai red curry paste i used 2
- 2 tablespoons 1-2 garam masala i used 1
- 1 teaspoon turmeric
- 2 teaspoons cayenne pepper or to taste
- 1/2 teaspoon salt
- 2 teaspoons saffron optional
- 2 cups 1-2 broccoli florets
- chopped cilantro for topping
- steamed rice for serving
- fresh naan for serving

DIRECTIONS

1. Heat a huge skillet over medium temperature and add 1 tablespoon coconut essential oil (or ghee). Once popular, add the cubed paneer in batches and make about 2 minutes per part or until sharp. Remove from heat and drain in writing towels. Do it again with any staying paneer. Reserve the skillet and arrange the paneer apart.*

2. To a food processor chip or high powered blender, add the cashews and coconut milk. Mix on high until totally smooth and silky, about 3-4 mins. Add the tomato paste, yogurt, and 1/2 cup water. Mix until smooth. Reserve.

3. To the same skillet, you fried the paneer, add the rest of the tablespoon of oil. Once popular, add the onion, garlic, and ginger, cook about 5-8 mins or before the onion is smooth and gently caramelized. Add the curry powder, thai reddish colored curry paste, garam masala, turmeric, cayenne, and salt. Cook about a minute and then mix in the cashew/coconut blend. Bring the sauce to a mild boil and if it appears too solid for your liking, mix in drinking water or coconut milk to slim. Once the sauce reaches your desired consistency, mix in the crispy paneer and saffron if using. Add the broccoli and make until warmed through and the sauce thickened somewhat about five minutes. Remove from heat and serve over a bed of warm rice sprinkled with cut cilantro. Also, keep in mind the naan for dipping!

PORK VINDALOO

Servings: 12

INGREDIENTS

- 1 1/2 cups 12-14 garlic
- 2 tbsp. hot paprika
- 2 tbsp. sugar
- 2 tbsp. sweet paprika
- 2 teaspoons brown mustard seeds

- 1 1/2 tablespoons kosher salt
- 4 tbsp. tomato paste
- 1 cup distilled white vinegar
- 1/2 cup canola oil
- 2 medium red onions, chopped (1 1/2 cups)
- 1 teaspoon crushed red chile flakes
- 4 pounds . pork shoulder, cut into 1/2-inch pieces (5 cups)

DIRECTIONS

1. Make the sauce: In a meals processor chip or blender, combine the garlic, both paprikas, mustard seeds, sugars, salt, tomato paste, vinegar, and 1/4 glass water; purée until soft.

2. In a sizable cast-iron skillet, heat the oil over medium-high. Add the onion and chile flakes, and make, stirring, before the onion is golden dark brown, about 5-6 mins. Add the pork and the puréed sauce. Stir well to layer the pork, cover, decrease temperature to low, and make before pork is falling aside and the sauce is usually solid and lush about 45 minutes.

REBECCA COLLERTON

Servings: 10

INGREDIENTS

- olive oil
- 12 scallions, cut into 1-inch pieces
- 4 jalapeños, seeds removed if desired
- 2 1-inch piece ginger, peeled, chopped
- 2 tablespoons fresh lemon juice
- 12 garlic cloves
- 2 tablespoons garam masala
- 2 teaspoons ground coriander
- 1 teaspoon ground cumin
- 1 teaspoon cayenne pepper
- 4 pounds ground beef (20% fat)
- 2 large eggs, beaten to blend
- 6 tablespoons plain yogurt
- 1 1/2 tablespoons kosher salt
- 1/2 cup olive oil
- 8 medium onions, chopped
- 20 garlic cloves, crushed

- 2 1/2-inch piece ginger, peeled, chopped
- 6 dried chiles de árbol
- 2 1/2 tablespoons curry powder
- 2 1/2 tablespoons ground cumin
- 2 1/2 tablespoons ground turmeric
- 6 tablespoons ground coriander
- 2 teaspoons black peppercorns
- 2 ounces 14.5- can crushed tomatoes
- 2 bay leaves
- 2 tablespoons kosher salt, plus more
- 2 tablespoons fresh lemon juice
- 1 teaspoon cayenne pepper
- leaf cilantro with tender stems (for serving)

DIRECTIONS

1. Preheat oven to 400°. Gently brush a rimmed baking sheet with essential oil. Purée scallions, jalapeños, garlic, ginger, lemon juice, garam masala, coriander, cumin, and cayenne in a blender until clean. Transfer blend to a huge bowl and put beef, egg, yogurt, and salt. Mix together with your hands until the blend is homogenous and begins to become extremely sticky like sausage meats, about 1 minute. Utilizing a 2-oz. ice cream scoop to part if you want, roll beef blend into golfing ball-size portions and put on a baking sheet, spacing 1" apart (you ought to have about 24). Drizzle meatballs with an increase of essential oil and bake until browned at the top and cooked through, 20-25 minutes.

2. Meanwhile, heat essential oil in a huge Dutch oven or additional heavy pot over moderate. Add onions, garlic, and ginger and prepare, stirring frequently, until onions are translucent and beginning to brown, 8-10 minutes. Mix in chiles, curry powder, cumin, turmeric, coriander, and peppercorns. Cook, stirring frequently until mixture is quite fragrant and spices start to adhere to the pot, about 2 mins. Add tomatoes, stirring and scraping bottom level of the pot, and provide to a boil. Add bay leaf, 1 Tbsp. salt, and 2 cups water; go back to a boil. Reduce temperature and simmer until tastes have melded, 25-30 minutes.

3. Let curry sauce awesome slightly, after transfer to a blender; blend until very clean. Get rid of any bits staying in the pot and transfer curry sauce back again to the pot. Mix in lemon juice and cayenne; flavor sauce and time of year with an increase of salt if needed.

4. Lightly nestle cooked meatballs into sauce, bring to a simmer, and cook until meatballs are heated completely, 10-15 minutes. Serve topped with cilantro.

5. Do Forward: Meatballs and sauce could be made one day ahead. Let great; transfer to an airtight container and chill. Carefully reheat meatballs in sauce, covered, thinning with drinking water if the sauce is normally too thick.

SAAG PANEER

Servings: 8

INGREDIENTS

- 16 cups milk
- 12 tbsp. ghee or canola oil
- 1/2 cup garlic, chopped
- 1/2 cup fresh lemon juice
- one 1-inch piece ginger, peeled and chopped
- 2 serrano chile, stemmed and chopped
- 12 cups finely chopped spinach
- kosher salt
- 12 tbsp. heavy cream
- 1 teaspoon garam masala
- 1/2 teaspoon cayenne
- indian flatbread or rice, for serving

DIRECTIONS

1. Make the cheese: Range a colander with 8 layers of cheesecloth, draping it over the sides, and occur a sink. In a big, nonstick pot over medium-high warmth, provide the milk to a complete boil, stirring frequently with a wooden spoon to avoid it from scorching underneath. Mix in the lemon juice, then lower heat to medium-low and prepare without stirring simply until large curds form about 30 secs. Remove from heat and reserve, without disturbing for 2 minutes, after that pour the milk mix into the colander. Collect the corners of cheesecloth jointly and carefully squeeze out a few of the surplus liquid. Tie the contrary corners of the cheesecloth jointly to produce a sack, and hang it from a sizable kitchen spoon suspended over a deep bowl. Reserve at room temperature before the excess liquid has completely drained from the cheese, about 1 1/2 hours. Transfer the sack to a plate, untie the cheesecloth, and loosely drape the corners over the cheese. Place a sizable heavy pot along with the cheese, then reserve at room temperatures to compress for thirty minutes more. Take away the pot and unwrap the cheese. Cut into 1/2-inch-by-1-inch parts.

2. In a 12-inch nonstick skillet, heat the ghee over medium. Employed in batches, add the cheese and fry until golden dark brown, about 6 minutes. Utilizing a slotted spoon, transfer the cheese to a plate and reserve; reserve the skillet with ghee.

3. Make the spinach: In a blender, combine the garlic, ginger, chile, and 1/4 cup drinking water; purée into a simple paste. Come back the skillet with ghee to the stove, and warmth over medium-high. Add the ginger-garlic paste and make, stirring, until fragrant, about 30 mere seconds. Add the spinach, salt to flavor, and cook, stirring frequently, before spinach wilts, about 1 minute. Decrease the warmth to

medium-low, cover, and cook, stirring often, before spinach is quite soft, about quarter-hour. Mix in the cream, garam masala, and cayenne. Add the cheese to the skillet, cover, and continue cooking food before liquid thickens and spinach is definitely soft, about a quarter-hour even more. Serve with flatbread or rice.

RICK MARTINEZ

Servings: 10

INGREDIENTS

- cup yogurt ½ whole-milk Greek yogurt
- 1/2 cup garlic grated
- 2 tablespoons ginger finely grated ginger
- 1 1/2 tablespoons salt kosher salt
- 2 tablespoons fenugreek leaves (optional)
- 4 pounds chicken thighs boneless skinless chicken thighs
- cup butter ½ (1 stick) cultured or unsalted butter divided
- 1 cup cinnamon 3-inch cinnamon
- 10 cardamom green cardamom pods
- 2 whole clove
- 1 1/2 tablespoons fenugreek seeds (optional)
- 4 onions medium onions sliced
- 4 serrano chiles split lengthwise
- salt Kosher salt
- 1/2 cup garlic grated
- 2 tablespoons ginger finely grated ginger
- 2 tablespoons fenugreek leaves (optional)
- 2 tablespoons garam masala
- 2 teaspoons paprika
- teaspoon turmeric ½ ground turmeric
- 4 cans tomatoes 28-ounce whole peeled tomatoes
- cup heavy cream ½ heavy cream
- cilantro Chopped cilantro steamed basmati rice and naan (for serving)

DIRECTIONS

1. Whisk yogurt, garlic, fenugreek leaves, if using, ginger, and salt in a moderate bowl. Add poultry and toss to layer. Cover and chill for at least one hour or more to 3.
2. Melt 4 Tbsp. butter in a sizable wide pot over moderate heat. Make cinnamon, cardamom pods, clove,

and fenugreek seeds, if using, stirring, until somewhat darker and fragrant, 1-2 mins. Add onion and chiles, period with salt, and make, stirring sometimes, until onion can be golden and starting to caramelize, 8-10 mins. Add garlic and ginger and prepare, stirring, until extremely fragrant and ginger begins to carefully turn golden and sticks to bottom level of the pot, 2-3 mins. Add fenugreek leaves, if using, garam masala, paprika, and turmeric and prepare, stirring, until extremely fragrant, about 1 minute. Add tomatoes, splitting up into parts with a spoon, and prepare until brick reddish colored and the majority of the liquid can be evaporated for about 1 minute. Utilizing a potato masher or large spoon, smash tomatoes and continue steadily to simmer, uncovered, until sauce may be the consistency of a heavy ragù, 40-50 mins. Discard cinnamon stay (leave other entire spices).

3. Transfer blend to a blender and purée until even. Cut staying 4 Tbsp. butter into parts. Add butter and cream to blender and purée until creamy; period with salt. Come back sauce to the pot and provide to a simmer.

4. Meanwhile, preheat the broiler. Arrange chicken within a layer on a cable rack set in the foil-lined rimmed baking sheet. Broil until chicken begins to brown in areas (you won't be cooked through), 7-8 minutes per aspect. When cool more than enough to take care of, cut into ¾" parts. Add poultry to simmering sauce, cover, and cook until poultry is cooked through, 8-10 minutes.

5. Best chicken and sauce with cilantro. Serve with rice and naan alongside.

6. Do Ahead: Butter poultry can be produced 3 days forward. Let great; cover and chill.

ROASTED EGGPLANT AND CRISPY KALE WITH YOGURT

Servings: 10

INGREDIENTS

*   4 medium italian eggplants (about 1 1/2 pounds total), quartered lengthwise, cut crosswise into 1-inch pieces
*   1/2 cup vegetable oil
*   kosher salt
*   1 teaspoon ground cumin
*   12 tuscan kale leaves, ribs and stems removed, leaves coarsely torn
*   2 teaspoons dried mangos powder (amchoor; optional)
*   2 medium persian cucumbers
*   2 cups plain whole-milk greek yogurt
*   2 teaspoons fresh lemon juice
*   2 garlic cloves, finely grated
*   4 cups cherry tomatoes, halved

- olive oil (for drizzling)

DIRECTIONS

1. Preheat oven to 450°. Toss eggplants with veggie essential oil on a rimmed baking sheet; time of year with salt. Roast, tossing halfway through, until eggplants are charred in places and tender, 20-25 moments. Remove from oven, sprinkle with mango powder (if using) and cumin, and toss to coat.

2. Meanwhile, heat a dry out a large skillet, ideally cast iron, over medium-large. Add kale, arranging to squeeze in an individual even layer (function in batches if required), and cook, turning sometimes until charred in places and crisp, about 4 minutes.

3. Grate cucumber about the moderate holes of a box grater; squeeze out extra liquid together with your hands and transfer to a moderate bowl. Blend in yogurt, lemon juice, and garlic; time of year with salt.

4. Toss tomatoes with an excellent pinch of salt and a drizzle of essential olive oil in a moderate bowl. Spoon yogurt combination onto a platter and coating eggplants, kale, and tomatoes at the top. Drizzle with even more olive oil.

ROTI (INDIAN WHOLE WHEAT FLATBREAD)

Servings: 11

INGREDIENTS

- 2 cups atta (chapati) flour, plus more for rolling
- 1/2 teaspoon kosher salt
- 3/4 teaspoon . corn oils or canola oil, plus more for shaping
- melted ghee, for brushing

DIRECTIONS

1. In a moderate bowl, use the hands to mix the flour, oil, and salt. Add 1 glass water and combine, pinching and kneading the dough as you function. Add yet another 1/4 cup of drinking water and continue steadily to knead and convert the dough in the bowl, scraping up the loose flour from the sides and bottom level. Continue before dough is smooth no much longer sticky. (If the dough appears dry, soon add up to 1/4 cup more drinking water, 1 tablespoon at the same time, blending well between each addition.)

2. Divide the dough into 4 equal parts. Rub a little of essential oil on your own hands, and roll each piece right into a log, about 2 inches heavy. Pinch off golf ball-sized pieces, about 1 1/4 ounce each, and roll each right into a ball. Cover the balls with a dish towel and reserve.

3. Fill a little bowl with atta flour, then lightly dirt a chakra or countertop with more flour. Dealing with one ball of dough at the same time, flatten the ball right into a thick disk. Dredge the disk of dough in the plate of flour, then make use of a belan or rolling pin to roll the ball right into a disc about 6-6 1/2 inches in diameter.

4. Meanwhile, at high temperature, a Tava or a moderate nonstick or cast iron dry out skillet over moderate to medium-high high temperature. When the pan is quite scorching, place one roti in the skillet. When you find small white spots type on the top of the dough, about 45 seconds, make use of tongs or your fingertips to flip, then make on the remaining aspect until it bubbles just a little and light brown areas form, 20-30 secs more.

5. Take away the roti from the pan and stick it directly over the gas flame; let make until it puffs and swells, after that, using tongs, quickly flip it backward and forwards for some seconds to keep puffing and getting brownish spots all over.

6. Transfer the roti to a serving dish and instantly brush 1 or both sides with ghee. Cover with a clean kitchen towel when you continue rolling and cooking food all of that other roti this way. Serve warm.

SAMBAR (SOUTH INDIAN VEGETABLE STEW)

Servings: 12

INGREDIENTS

- 1 cup toor dal (yellow pigeon peas), rinsed, soaked 30 minutes, and drained
- 1 cup coconut or canola oil
- 2 small red onions, cut into 1" pieces
- 2 pieces 1 (2") ginger, peeled and mashed into a paste
- 1 cup garlic, mashed into a paste
- 8 small green thai chiles or 2 serranos, chopped
- 4 drumsticks, trimmed and cut into 2" pieces
- 4 medium carrots, quartered lengthwise and cut into 2" pieces
- 4 medium yukon gold potatoes, peeled and cut into 1" pieces
- 4 plum tomatoes, chopped
- 1 cup sambar masala
- 6 tbsp. fresh or frozen grated coconut
- 6 tbsp. tamarind paste
- 2 tbsp. ground cumin
- 2 teaspoons ground turmeric
- 20 small okra, trimmed and halved crosswise
- kosher salt, to taste
- 1 1/2 tablespoons black mustard seeds
- 20 fresh or frozen curry leaves
- 10 chiles de árbol

- 1/2 cup cilantro leaves
- cooked white rice, for serving (optional)

DIRECTIONS

1. Bring 1/3 glass toor dal and 4 cups drinking water to a boil in a 6-qt. saucepan. Reduce heat to moderate and make until dal is quite tender about one hour. Transfer to a bowl; reserve.
2. Wipe pan clean; temperature half the essential oil over medium-high. Make garlic, onion, and ginger until slightly caramelized, 8-10 mins. Add green chiles, drumsticks, carrots, potatoes, tomatoes, and 3 1/2 cups water; boil. Reduce temperature to moderate; simmer until vegetables are tender, 15-20 mins. Mix in reserved toor dal, the sambar masala, coconut, tamarind paste, cumin, turmeric, okra, and salt; simmer until okra is definitely tender, 10-15 minutes.
3. Heat remaining oil within an 8" skillet over medium-high; prepare mustard seeds, curry leaves, and chiles de árbol until seeds pop, 1-2 mins; pour over the sambar and garnish with cilantro. Serve with rice privately if you like.

TANDOORI CHICKEN DRUMSTICKS WITH CILANTRO-SHALLOT RELISH

Servings: 10

INGREDIENTS

- 2 tablespoons sweet paprika
- 2 tablespoons garam masala
- 2 tablespoons ground cumin
- 1 teaspoon ground turmeric
- 2 tablespoons finely grated peeled fresh ginger
- 2 tablespoons ground coriander
- 1/2 cup garlic
- 1/2 cup fat-free greek-style yogurt
- 2 tablespoons lemon juice
- 1 cup canola oil
- kosher salt
- freshly ground pepper
- 24 chicken drumsticks
- 1 1/2 cups coarsely chopped cilantro
- 2 small shallots
- 6 tablespoons distilled white vinegar

DIRECTIONS

1. Preheat the oven to 450 degrees F. Established a rack on each of 2 large baking sheets. In a little skillet, toast the paprika, garam masala, cumin, coriander, and turmeric over moderately low high temperature, stirring, until fragrant, about 2 a few minutes. Transfer the spices to a moderate bowl and cool somewhat. Mix in the ginger, garlic, yogurt, lemon juice, and 2 tablespoons of the essential oil and period with salt and pepper. Make two or three 3 slashes in each drumstick. In a sizable bowl, toss the poultry with 2 tablespoons of the canola essential oil and period with salt and pepper. Add the spiced yogurt and rub it onto the poultry. Arrange the poultry on the racks, departing 2 inches between your pieces. Roast for 45 minutes, turning occasionally before the chicken is golden dark brown, and prepared through. Light the broiler and broil the poultry 6 inches from heat for about five minutes, until gently charred and sharp. In a little bowl, mix the cilantro, shallot, vinegar, and the rest of the 1/4 glass of oil; time of year with salt. Serve with the poultry. Looking for more poultry recipes? Try our selections of chicken white meat recipes, chicken casserole quality recipes, and quality recipes for leftover chicken.

SPICED DAL WITH PEANUTS AND DILL

Servings: 8

INGREDIENTS

- 12 tbsp. split yellow lentils
- 1/2 cup vegetable oil
- 20 garlic cloves, minced
- 4 small green indian chiles or serranos, stemmed, seeded, and minced
- 1 1/2 tablespoons whole cumin seeds
- 4 small red onions, minced
- 4 medium plum tomatoes, cored and finely chopped
- 2 tbsp. ground coriander
- 2 teaspoons ground turmeric
- 2 teaspoons red kashmiri chile powder
- 6 cups roughly chopped dill
- 1 cup finely chopped peanuts
- kosher salt

DIRECTIONS

1. In a bowl, cover the lentils with water, let them soak for thirty minutes, and drain. In a 12-in. skillet, warm the essential oil over medium-high warmth. Add the cumin seeds and make, stirring continuously, until fragrant, about 1 minute. Add the garlic, chiles, and onions and make, stirring, before onions are smooth and golden brown, about 12 minutes.

2. Mix in the tomatoes, make for 2 minutes, in that case, put the coriander, turmeric, and chile powder and

make, stirring, until fragrant, about 2 minutes. Mix the lentils, dill, peanuts, and 1 1/2 cups drinking water, and prepare, stirring, before dal is tender, about 20 minutes. Time of year the dal with salt and serve while warm.

THALASSERY MEEN CURRY (THALASSERY-STYLE FISH CURRY)

Servings: 4

INGREDIENTS

- 2 pounds . skin-on mackerel steaks, pin bones removed
- kosher salt, to taste
- 1 teaspoon ground turmeric
- 8 chiles de árbol
- 2 cups freshly grated coconut
- 6 tbsp. coconut or canola oil
- 10 small green thai chiles or 2 1/2 serranos, halved
- 4 plum tomatoes, chopped
- 2 green, unripe mangos, peeled, pitted, and minced
- 2 pieces 1 (2") ginger, peeled and minced
- 24 fresh or frozen curry leaves
- cooked white rice, for serving (optional)

DIRECTIONS

1. Season seafood with salt; reserve. Purée coconut, turmeric, and chiles de árbol in a little food processor right into a paste; set aside.
2. High-temperature oil in a 12" skillet more than medium-high; prepare green chiles, tomatoes, mango, and ginger, stirring sometimes, until tomatoes start to breakdown and mango is certainly tender, 8-10 a few minutes. Add reserved coconut paste and 1 cup drinking water; boil. Add seafood; cook until seafood is cooked through, 6-8 minutes. Mix in curry leaves; serve with rice privately if you like.

SAMBAR MASALA

Servings: 4

INGREDIENTS

- 4 tbsp. canola oil
- 1 cup urad dal (skinned split black lentils)
- 2/3 cup masoor dal (split red lentils)

- 1/2 cup coriander seeds
- 1/2 cup chana dal (yellow split peas)
- 3 tbsp. sesame seeds
- 1 tablespoon . asafoetida
- 1 tablespoon . cumin seeds
- 44 fresh or frozen curry leaves
- 20 chiles de árbol
- 1 tablespoon . fenugreek seeds
- 6 tbsp. kosher salt
- 3 cups roasted chana dal

DIRECTIONS

1. High-temperature oil in a 12" skillet over medium-high. Make dals, stirring sometimes, until golden, 3-4 a few minutes. Add coriander and sesame seeds, asafoetida, cumin seeds, curry leaves, and chiles; prepare until fragrant and chiles certainly are a deep reddish-brown, 3-4 a few minutes. Stir in fenugreek seeds and salt; cook 30 seconds even more and let great. Stir in roasted chana dal and, employed in batches, transfer to a spice grinder; grind to a powder. Store within an airtight container for 3 months.

VEGETARIAN CURRY WITH CABBAGE AND POTATOES

Servings: 8

INGREDIENTS

- 6 tbsp. canola oil
- 1 tablespoon . cumin seeds
- 1 teaspoon ground turmeric
- 6 small green thai chiles or 1 serrano, sliced 1/2" thick
- 1 teaspoon red chile powder, such as cayenne
- 4 indian or regular bay leaves
- 2 small red onions, quartered and cut into 1/4" wedges
- 3 pounds . yukon gold potatoes, peeled, quartered, and sliced 1/4" thick
- 8 plum tomatoes, chopped
- 1 small head green cabbage, cored and cut into 1" pieces
- kosher salt, to taste

DIRECTIONS

1. High-temperature oil in a 12" skillet over medium-high. Make cumin seeds until they pop, 1-2 a few minutes. Add chile powder, turmeric, chiles, bay leaves, and onion; prepare until onion is gentle, 3-4

minutes. Mix in potatoes, tomatoes, cabbage, and salt; make, protected, until potatoes are tender, about thirty minutes.

SOUTH INDIAN PEPPER CHICKEN CURRY

Servings: 8

INGREDIENTS

- 2 (2 1/2–3-lb.) chicken or 2-lb. boneless, skinless chicken thighs
- 1/2 cup canola oil
- 3 tbsp. cumin seeds
- 1 tablespoon . fennel seeds
- 6 tbsp. coriander seeds
- 1 tablespoon . urad dal (skinned split black lentils), rinsed, soaked 30 minutes, and drained
- 20 fresh or frozen curry leaves
- 6 indian or regular bay leaves
- 6 whole cloves
- 1 cup cinnamon, halved
- 2 teaspoons ground cardamom
- 1 teaspoon ground turmeric
- 2/3 cup garlic, mashed into a paste
- 2 large yellow onions, minced
- 2 pieces 1 (2") ginger, peeled and mashed into a paste
- kosher salt, to taste
- 4 plum tomatoes, minced
- 3 tbsp. coarsely ground black pepper
- 1/2 cup chopped cilantro
- cooked white rice, for serving (optional)

DIRECTIONS

1. Separate chicken into 8 pieces. Cut drumsticks, thighs, and wings in two; slice breasts crosswise into thirds-you could have 18 bits of chicken.

2. Warmth oil in a 12" nonstick skillet more than medium-high. Make coriander, cumin, and fennel seeds, dal, curry and bay leaves, cloves, and cinnamon until dal are golden, 2-3 moments. Stir in cardamom, turmeric, garlic, onion, and ginger; cook until somewhat caramelized, 6-8 moments. Add tomatoes; prepare until divided, 4-5 moments. Add chicken and 1/2 cup drinking water; boil. Reduce warmth to medium-low; make, covered, until poultry is cooked through, about 25 moments. Uncover and increase warmth to medium-high. Stir in pepper; simmer until somewhat thickened, 3-4 moments. Garnish with

cilantro; serve with rice if you want.

PISTACHIO ICE CREAM

Servings: 5

INGREDIENTS

- 1/16 teaspoon saffron threads
- 4 tbsp. sugar
- 4 cups whole milk
- cardamom seeds from 2 pods, crushed
- 2 tbsp. finely chopped pistachios

DIRECTIONS

1. Temperature 8 cups milk in a 6-qt. Dutch oven over medium-high temperature, stirring continuously until it simply reaches a boil. Mix in saffron, reduce temperature to low, and lightly simmer milk, stirring sometimes, until reduced to 3 cups, about 4 hours. Remove pan from temperature and whisk in the sugar and crushed cardamom seeds; let awesome to room temperature.
2. Mix in pistachios. Pour blend into 10 paper cups or kulfi molds. Freeze for 6 hours or until set. To provide, pinch molds release a kulfi onto plates.

THE BON APPÉTIT TEST KITCHEN

Servings: 10

INGREDIENTS

- 2 onions, chopped
- 2 garlic cloves, sliced
- 1/4 cup vegetable oil
- 4 cardamom pods
- 1/4 cup chopped peeled ginger
- 2 teaspoons curry powder
- 2 ounces 28- can peeled whole tomatoes with their juices, crushed
- 2 ounces 15- can chickpeas, rinsed
- kosher salt and freshly ground black pepper
- cooked basmati rice (for serving)
- chopped fresh cilantro (for serving)

DIRECTIONS

1. Make onion, garlic, and ginger in essential oil with cardamom and curry powder until onion is soft, 8-10 mins. Add tomatoes with their juices and chickpeas and simmer until gentle, 25-30 minutes; period with

salt and pepper. Serve with rice and cilantro.

ZOOMRU TOOL AND RUWANGAN HACH (FRIED HARD-BOILED EGGS WITH OVEN-DRIED TOMATOES)

Servings: 4

INGREDIENTS

- 12 plum tomatoes, cored and halved lengthwise
- 4 tbsp. canola oil
- kosher salt, to taste
- 12 eggs, room temperature
- 2 teaspoons ground turmeric
- 4 small asian shallots s or 1 regular shallot, minced
- 1/2 cup mustard or canola oil
- 2 small red onions, minced
- 1 teaspoon kashmiri chile paste or 1 1/2 tsp. red chile powder or cayenne
- 2 teaspoons ground fennel
- 6 tablespoons garlic, mashed into a paste
- 2 pieces 1 (1") ginger, mashed into a paste
- chapati or naan bread, for serving (optional)

DIRECTIONS

1. Heat oven to 300°. Toss tomatoes with canola essential oil and salt; spread lower side through to a baking sheet. Make until dried out but nonetheless a little juicy, about 2 1/2 hours.
2. Bring 8 cups of drinking water to a boil in a 4-qt. saucepan. Add eggs; prepare until gentle- to medium-boiled (whites ought to be company and yolks somewhat runny), 6-7 minutes. Utilizing a slotted spoon, transfer eggs to an ice bath until chilled, then lightly peel.
3. Heat mustard essential oil in a 12" skillet over medium-high. Add turmeric and eggs; cook, lightly turning eggs until golden in color, 2-3 minutes. Utilizing a slotted spoon; transfer eggs to a bowl.
4. Make shallots and onion until slightly caramelized, 10-12 minutes. Mix in chile paste, fennel, garlic, and ginger; prepare until fragrant, 1-2 mins. Add reserved tomatoes and 1/2 cup drinking water; simmer, stirring sometimes, until tomatoes are divided and sauce is certainly thickened, 8-10 mins. Add reserved eggs; prepare until heated through, 1-2 mins. Serve with a loaf of bread, if you like.

ABRAHAM CONLON AND ADRIENNE LO

Servings: 10

INGREDIENTS

- 1 teaspoon kosher salt plus more
- 2 pieces ” ginger, peeled
- 2 tbsp. olive oil
- 2 teaspoons yellow mustard seeds
- 1 medium head cauliflower, cut into small florets
- 2 teaspoons fennel seeds
- 2 teaspoons ground coriander
- 2 teaspoons ground cumin
- 2 teaspoons ground turmeric
- 1/2 cup fresh lime juice
- leaf cilantro with tender stems (for serving)

DIRECTIONS

1. Toss jalapeño and ½ tsp. salt in a little bowl. Finely grate ginger and squeeze the juice into jalapeño mixture (you ought to have about 1 Tbsp. juice); discard pulp. Arranged jalapeño mixture aside.
2. Make cauliflower in a moderate pot of boiling salted drinking water until the tops of the florets are slightly translucent, about 1 minute; drain and rinse under cool water. Set aside.
3. Cook essential oil and mustard seeds in a moderate saucepan over medium-high warmth, stirring, until seeds start to pop, about 2 moments. Add fennel seeds, coriander, cumin, and turmeric. Make, stirring, until fragrant, about 1 minute. Remove saucepan from the warmth and blend in lime juice and reserved jalapeño combination. Let cool; time of year with salt. Add reserved cauliflower to the saucepan and allow marinate at least one hour.
4. Top with cilantro right before serving.
5. DO AHEAD: Cauliflower could be made 3 times ahead. Cover and chill.

SIMPLE KHICHARI

Servings: 5

INGREDIENTS

- 1/4 cup red split lentils
- 1/4 cup yellow split mung dal
- 1/4 cup white quinoa
- 2 tablespoons ghee or melted virgin coconut oils
- 1/4 cup basmati rice
- 1/2 teaspoon ground turmeric

- 6 fresh curry leaves or 2 dried cassia leaves (optional)
- 1 1-inch piece ginger, peeled, very finely chopped (about 1 tablespoon)
- 1 small green thai chile, finely chopped
- 2 cups chopped cauliflower florets and/or peeled daikon
- 1 teaspoon ground fennel seeds
- 1 teaspoon (or more) himalayan rock salt (or kosher salt)
- cilantro, basil, lime slices, black pepper, and olive oil (for serving)

DIRECTIONS

1. Cover lentils and mung dal with drinking water in a little bowl and permit soak thirty minutes. Drain. Meanwhile, wash rice and quinoa and drain well.

2. Temperature ghee in a huge pot more than medium-low. Add turmeric and toast simply until slightly darkened, about 10 mere seconds. Add curry leaves, if using, ginger, and chile and cook until extremely fragrant, about 1 minute. Add drained lentils, mung dal, rice, and quinoa and make, stirring, until almost dry, 1-2 mins. Add cauliflower, fennel seeds, 1 tsp. salt, and 4 cups water. Boost heat to medium-high and provide to a boil. Reduce temperature and skim off any foam that shaped on the surface, after that simmer protected until grains and vegetables are extremely tender, 30-40 mins; the khichari ought to be thick, very smooth, and just lose plenty of not to adhere to bottom level of the pot (add water as had a need to loosen). Season with an increase of salt, if needed.

3. Divide among bowls. Best with cilantro, basil, dark pepper, and limes. Drizzle with oil.

DAI DUE, AUSTIN, TX

Servings: 10

INGREDIENTS

- cup yogurt ½ plain whole-milk yogurt
- cup hot sauce ¼ vinegar-based hot sauce (such as Crystal)
- 1/4 cup olive oil olive oil
- 2 tablespoons oregano finely chopped fresh oregano
- 2 teaspoons black pepper freshly ground black pepper
- 1/2 cup garlic finely chopped garlic
- teaspoon ½ garam masala
- 2 chicken Dai Due's Master Brined Chicken backbone removed
- vegetable oil Vegetable oil (for grilling)

DIRECTIONS

1. Combine yogurt, hot sauce, essential olive oil, garlic, oregano, pepper, and garam masala in a sizable resealable plastic handbag. Add poultry, backbone removed, and convert to coat. Seal handbag, pressing out surroundings; chill chicken 8-24 hours.

2. Prepare grill for moderate heat; lightly brush grate with veggie oil. Remove poultry from marinade, wiping off any unwanted, and grill, skin aspect down, until epidermis is normally lightly charred and releases from grate without tearing, 10-15 a few minutes. Give bird 25 % turn and continue steadily to grill until epidermis is properly charred and sharp and thighs are needs to firm up (they must be springy when pressed), 15-20 minutes. Turn the poultry over and grill until an instant-read thermometer inserted into the thickest component of the thigh registers 165°, 10-15 minutes.

3. Place chicken in a platter skin aspect up; let rest ten minutes before carving.

MONICA BHIDE

Servings: 10

INGREDIENTS

- 16 whole cloves
- 4 small dried chiles (such as chiles de árbol), stemmed
- 2 teaspoons cumin seeds
- 1/2 teaspoon whole black peppercorns
- 1 1/2 tablespoons fennel seeds
- 2/3 cup whole-milk plain yogurt
- 1 1/2 tablespoons finely grated peeled fresh ginger
- 16 lamb rib chops (each about 1 inch thick), excess fat trimmed
- pickled red onion (click for recipe)
- fresh mint sprigs (for garnish)

DIRECTIONS

1. Combine the first 5 elements in a small skillet. Mix over medium warmth until spices are aromatic and somewhat darker in color, about three minutes. Transfer spices to a bowl and awesome. Grind spices to a coarse powder in a spice mill. Combine spices, yogurt, and ginger in a 11x7x2-inch cup baking dish. Add lamb chops and change to coat with the combination. Let marinate for thirty minutes.

2. Preheat broiler. Collection rimmed baking sheet with foil. Arrange chops on the baking sheet. Broil lamb to preferred doneness, about three minutes per part for medium-rare. Transfer 2 lamb chops to each of 4 plates. Spoon drained Pickled Crimson Onions together with each; garnish with mint sprigs.

CROCK-POT BUTTER CHICKEN

Servings: 10

INGREDIENTS

- 4 pounds . boneless skinless chicken breasts, cut into 1" pieces
- 2 onions, chopped

- 6 tablespoons garlic, minced
- 2 tablespoons freshly grated ginger
- 2 teaspoons turmeric
- 4 jalapeños, minced
- 2 teaspoons cumin
- 2 teaspoons garam masala
- kosher salt
- 2 cups greek yogurt
- 2 cans -oz. plus 1 14-oz. can diced tomatoes
- 1/2 cup butter
- 1/2 cup heavy cream
- 1/4 cup chopped cilantro, for garnish
- naan, for serving
- cooked basmati rice, for serving

DIRECTIONS

1. On the plate of the Crock-Pot, toss together chicken, onion, garlic, jalapeños, ginger, turmeric, cumin, garam masala, and 3/4 teaspoon kosher salt. Add Greek yogurt and toss before the chicken mixture is covered. Pour tomatoes at the top and stir softly to mix, then dot best with butter. Make on low before poultry is cooked through, 6 to 7 hours. Switch off warmth and uncover Crock-Pot. Mix in heavy cream after that season to flavor with an increase of salt, if required. Garnish with cilantro. Serve warm with naan and rice.

NAAN (INDIAN LEAVENED FLATBREAD)

Servings: 5

INGREDIENTS

- 6 tablespoons water heated to 115°
- 1/2 teaspoon honey
- 1/2 package 1 (1/4-oz.) active dry yeast
- 1/4 cup plain, full-fat greek yogurt
- 1 tbsp. canola oil
- 1 cup all-purpose flour
- 1/4 teaspoon kosher salt
- 2 tablespoons minced cilantro
- melted ghee, for brushing

DIRECTIONS

1. Stir drinking water and honey in a bowl; add yeast and allow sit until foamy, about ten minutes. Add flour, yogurt, essential oil, and salt; mix until dough forms. Using hands, knead dough in the bowl until smooth, about five minutes. Cover dough with a damp cloth; let sit down in a warm place until doubled in proportions, about 1 hour.
2. Transfer dough to a function surface; divide into 10 balls. Dealing with 1 ball at the same time and utilizing a rolling pin, roll the dough right into a 7" circle about 1/4" heavy. Sprinkle with 1/4 tsp. cilantro; press into dough.
3. Heat a 12" nonstick skillet over medium-high. Dealing with 1 piece of dough at the same time, cook the dough, basic aspect down, until bubbles show up over the top, about 45 secs. Flip dough; prepare until bubbles show up once again, about 30 secs. Transfer naan to a plate and slide skillet off temperature. Using tongs, make naan about 2" over the open up flame, flipping once, until browned in spots, about 1 minute. (Alternatively, surface finishes cooking food naan in a pan until browned in areas, about 1 minute.) Come back naan to plate, brush with ghee, and sprinkle with an increase of cilantro. Serve hot.

CLAIRE SAFFITZ

Servings: 10

INGREDIENTS

- 4 garlic cloves finely grated, divided
- 1 cup plain whole-milk greek yogurt, divided
- 1/4 cup vadouvan
- 2/3 cup olive oils, divided
- kosher salt and freshly ground black pepper
- 2 pounds small carrots, tops trimmed, scrubbed
- 1/2 teaspoon ground turmeric
- 1/4 cup fresh lemon juice
- very coarsely chopped cilantro leaves with tender stems and lemon wedges (for serving)

DIRECTIONS

1. Preheat oven to 425°. Combine vadouvan, half of the garlic, ¼ cup yogurt, and 3 Tbsp. the essential oil in a sizable bowl until smooth; period with salt and pepper. Add carrots and toss to layer. Roast on a rimmed baking sheet within a layer, turning sometimes, until tender and gently charred in spots, 25-30 minutes.
2. Meanwhile, high-temperature turmeric and remain-ing 2 Tbsp. the essential oil in a little skillet over the medium-low, swirling skillet, until fragrant, about 2 a few minutes. Remove from heat.
3. Whisk lemon juice, remaining garlic, and remaining ¼ glass yogurt in a little bowl; period with salt and pepper.
4. Place carrots (along with crunchy bits on the baking sheet) on a platter. Drizzle with yogurt mix and

turmeric essential oil and best with cilantro. Serve with lemon wedges.

PARATHA (INDIAN LAYERED FLATBREAD)

Servings: 7
INGREDIENTS

- 2 cups atta (durum wheat flour), plus more for dusting
- melted ghee, for brushing

DIRECTIONS

1. Place 1/2 glass flour in a bowl; reserve. In another bowl, mix remaining flour and 1 1/4 cups drinking water until dough forms. Knead the dough briefly until easy, 1-2 moments; divide into fourteen 2-oz. balls.
2. Dealing with 1 ball of dough at the same time, dip the ball in reserved flour, and utilizing a rolling pin, roll right into a 5" circle about 1/8" solid. Fold the circle in two; brush with ghee. Fold in two again, making a little triangle; reroll right into a 5" triangle. Warmth a 12" cast-iron skillet over high.
3. Make the dough, flipping once, until puffed and golden, 1-2 moments. Transfer paratha to a plate and brush with an increase of ghee. Serve hot.

PANEER METHI CHEESE MARKECHILLA

Cooking time: 20 minutes - **Servings:** 2
INGREDIENTS:

- 7 oz paneer, cubed
- ½ onion, chopped
- 1 tomato, chopped
- ½ green chilli, chopped
- 1 garlic clove
- ½ teaspoon ginger paste
- 3 tablespoons heavy whipping cream
- 1 tablespoon butter
- 1/2 teaspoon cumin seeds
- 1 ½ teaspoon red chilli powder
- ½ teaspoon coriander powder
- 1 teaspoon turmeric powder
- 1 teaspoon garam masala

- ½ teaspoon dried kasuri methi leaves
- Fresh cilantro leaves, chopped, for serving
- Salt, to taste

DIRECTIONS

1. Season paneer with 1/2 teaspoon turmeric powder, salt and ½ teaspoon red chilli powder.
2. Preheat about 1 tablespoon butter in a skillet. Add paneer and cook for 2-3 minutes per side.
3. Preheat butter in a sauce pan, add cumin, ginger paste, green chilli, onions, garlic, tomato and cook for 2-3 minutes. Let cool and transfer the mixture to a blender, process until of a paste consistency.
4. Return the paste to the pan. Add turmeric powder, red chilli powder, coriander powder, garam masala and cook for 3-4 minutes.
5. Reduce the heat to low and add heavy whipping cream, stir well. Add cooked paneer, Kasuri methi leaves and simmer for 4-5 minutes.
6. Serve topped with cilantro and serve.

VEGGIE AND RICOTTA MUFFINS

Cooking time: 30minutes - **Servings:** 2

INGREDIENTS:

- 4 eggs
- 4 slices bacon, cooked and crumbled
- 1 tablespoon sundried tomato in olive oil, chopped
- 4 medium mushrooms, chopped
- 1 tablespoon fresh basil, chopped
- ¼ teaspoon onion salt
- ¼ teaspoon garlic opt, chopped
- ¼ cup parmesan, shredded
- ½ teaspoon Italian seasoning

DIRECTIONS

1. Preheat the oven to 400 F.
2. Spray muffin pan with cooking spray.
3. Mix all the ingredients in a bowl until well combined. Divide the batter among cups and bake for 25-30 minutes.
4. Let rest for couple of minutes before serving.

SPICY BACON AND EGG CUPS KETO

Cooking time: 30 minutes - **Servings:** 2

INGREDIENTS:

- 4 oz cheddar cheese, shredded
- 3 oz cream cheese
- 4 chili peppers, de-seeded and sliced
- 12 strips bacon
- 8 eggs, beaten
- ½ teaspoon garlic powder
- ½ teaspoon onion powder
- Salt and pepper, to taste

DIRECTIONS

1. Preheat the oven to 375F. Preheat a non stick skillet over medium heat. Add bacon and cook until slightly browned. Transfer to a plate.
2. Mix cream cheese, eggs, garlic powder, onion powder, salt and pepper in a bowl.
3. Prepare muffin tins and grease with cooking spray.
4. Par-cook bacon so it's semi crisp but still pliable. Save bacon grease to add to mixture.
5. Use a hand mixer, to mix all the other ingredients (except cheddar and 1 jalapeno) together.
6. Grease wells of muffin tin, then place cooked bacon around the edges. Pour the egg mixture into the muffin cups.
7. Top with cheddar cheese and chili pepper ring. Cook for 20-25 minutes. Let cool before serving.

BREAKFAST BOWL UPMA

Cooking time: 15 minutes - **Servings:** 2

INGREDIENTS:

- 7 oz cauliflower
- 2 tablespoons ghee
- 1 teaspoon ginger
- ½ onion
- 4 curry leaves
- 1 tablespoon cumin seeds
- 1 tablespoon mustard seeds
- 1 green chilly, chopped
- Chopped coriander, for serving
- Salt, to taste

DIRECTIONS

1. Add cauliflower florets to a food processor and blend to get rice consistency.

2. Preheat ghee in a deep skillet over medium heat. Add cumin and mustard seeds. Add onion, curry leaves, ginger and chilli, season with salt. Cook for about 3-4 minutes.

3. Add cauliflower rice and cook for 2 minutes. Add 1 cup water and cover the skillet, cook for 10 minutes, stirring from time to time.

4. Serve topped with coriander.

MEAT AND VEGGIE STUFFED OMELET

Cooking time: 5 minutes - **Servings:** 2

INGREDIENTS:

- 4 eggs
- 1 cup cooked chicken meat
- 1 cup frozen vegetables mix
- ¼ teaspoon salt
- ¼ teaspoon red chili powder
- 1 green chili, chopped
- ½ onion, chopped
- 1 teaspoon coriander
- 1 tablespoon butter
- A pinch of turmeric

DIRECTIONS

1. Beat eggs, salt, chilli powder, turmeric, coriander, onion and green chilli in a bowl.

2. Preheat butter in a skillet over medium heat. Add chicken and frozen vegetables, cook for about 3-4 minutes.

3. Add the beaten egg mixture, fry the eggs until set on one side. Fold the eggs and cook for about 2-3 minutes more. Enjoy!

BACON BRUSSELS SPROUTS

Cooking time: 15 minutes - **Servings:** 4

INGREDIENTS:

- 12 oz Brussels sprouts
- 4 slices bacon, chopped
- 2 garlic cloves
- 1 teaspoon paprika
- 1 tablespoon olive oil
- 1 teaspoon salt

- 1/2 teaspoon pepper

DIRECTIONS

1. Preheat a non stick skillet over medium heat. Add bacon and cook until slightly browned. Transfer to a plate.
2. Add olive oil to the skillet, add sprouts, salt, pepper and paprika. Cook for about 5 minutes. Add garlic and cook for 5 minutes more.
3. Add bacon to the skillet and cook for 1 minute. Serve.

CAULIFLOWER TIKKIS

Cooking time: 15 minutes - **Servings:** 4

INGREDIENTS:

- 8 cauliflower florets
- 1 onion, chopped
- 1/4 cup coriander leaves, chopped
- 2 green chilies, chopped
- 3 tablespoons gram flour
- 1 tablespoons coriander powder
- 1 teaspoon cumin powder
- 1/2 teaspoon black pepper
- 1/2 teaspoon turmeric powder
- 1 teaspoon red chili powder
- 4 tablespoons mustard oil
- Salt, to taste

DIRECTIONS

1. Bring a pan of water to a boil and add salt. Add cauliflower and simmer for 5-6 minutes. Drain and grate the florets to flour texture.
2. Add cauliflower, onion, coriander, green chilies, flour, coriander, cumin, turmeric, chili powder, salt and pepper to a bowl and mix well to combine.
3. Preheat oil in a skillet over medium heat. Shape the mixture into patties and fry in the skillet and fry until browned on both sides.

MULTI FILLINGS EGG MUFFINS

Cooking time: 25 minutes - **Servings:** 6

INGREDIENTS:

- 12 eggs

- 2 scallions, chopped
- 5 oz chorizo, cooked
- 6 oz cheese, shredded
- 2 tablespoons red pesto
- Salt and pepper, to taste

DIRECTIONS

1. Preheat the oven to 350°F. Prepare muffin tin and grease with cooking spray.
2. Mix all the batter ingredients in a bowl and divide among muffin cups.
3. Bake for 15-20 minutes.

CHEESE AND MEAT CHIPS

Cooking time: 10 minutes - **Servings:** 4

INGREDIENTS:

- 3 oz salami, 20 slices
- 4 oz parmesan cheese, grated
- 1 teaspoon paprika powder

DIRECTIONS

1. Preheat the oven to 450°F. Prepare a baking sheet and line it with parchment paper.
2. Place the salami slices on the baking sheet. Add the shredded cheese on top of each slice, sprinkle with paprika powder.
3. Bake until the cheese turns golden brown. Serve.

ROASTED MIXED NUTS

Cooking time: 5 minutes - **Servings:** 16

INGREDIENTS:

- 3 cups raw nuts (cashews, almonds and Brazil nuts)
- 1 teaspoon sea salt
- 1 tablespoon cinnamon
- 1 teaspoon vanilla essence
- 1 cup granulated Erythritol
- 1/4 cup water

DIRECTIONS

1. Preheat a deep pot over medium heat. Add Erythritol, sea salt, cinnamon and water and mix to combine. Heat up, stirring occasionally.
2. Add the nuts and mix to combine. Cook for about 2-3 minutes, stirring often.

3. Let rest for 1-2 minutes before serving.

KURKURE PANEER SLICES

Cooking time: 5 minutes - **Servings:** 8
INGREDIENTS:

- 3 ½ oz paneer, sliced
- 3 tablespoons breadcrumbs
- 2 tablespoons ground flaxseeds
- 1 teaspoon turmeric powder
- 2 teaspoons red chili powder
- 1 teaspoon cumin powder
- 1 teaspoon garam masala
- 1 teaspoon chat masala
- Salt, to taste
- Oil, for frying

DIRECTIONS

1. Toss paneer in 2 teaspoons corn flour and salt.
2. Mix flaxseeds, turmeric powder, red chilli powder, cumin powder, garam masala and salt in a bowl.
3. Add water and mix well until lump free batter is formed.
4. Preheat oil in a pan, dip each paneer slice into batter and then dip into breadcrumbs. Fry until brown on all sides.

CHEESY TAMATAR SALAD

Cooking time: 5 minutes - **Servings:** 2
INGREDIENTS:

- 1 cucumber, chopped
- 1 plum tomato, chopped
- 1 red onion, sliced
- 1 lime, juiced
- 3 oz paneer, cubed
- 2 green chillies
- 1 teaspoon chat masala
- Fresh chopped coriander

DIRECTIONS

1. Mix cucumber, tomato, onion and paneer in a bowl.

2. Add coriander and sprinkle with lime juice, toss to coat.

3. Add chat masala and stir to combine. Serve.

CRUNCHY BROCCOLI TOFU SALAD

Cooking time: 15 minutes - **Servings:** 4

INGREDIENTS:

- 1 (14 oz) package extra-firm tofu
- 1 head of broccoli, florets chopped
- 2 tablespoons vegetable oil
- 2 scallions, sliced
- 1 hot chili, sliced
- Salt and pepper, to taste

For the Dressing:

- 1 tablespoon rice vinegar
- ½ teaspoon soy sauce
- ¼ teaspoon sugar
- 2 tablespoons sesame oil
- 2 teaspoons sesame seeds, toasted

DIRECTIONS

1. Preheat the oven to 400 F. Toss broccoli florets with 1 tablespoon vegetable oil, salt and pepper. Place on a baking sheet and bake for about 5 minutes, remove from the oven. Reduce oven heat to 350 F.

2. Preheat the remaining oil in a pan. Add tofu and sprinkle with salt and pepper. Add to the pan and cook for about 1-2 minutes per all sides.

3. Transfer to the baking sheet and cook for 8-10 minutes.

4. Mix all dressing ingredients in a bowl. Mix broccoli, tofu, scallions and chili, top with dressing, toss to coat. Serve.

SAUSAGE STIR FRY

Cooking time: 25 minutes - **Servings:** 4

INGREDIENTS:

- 10 chicken sausages, sliced
- 2 tablespoons oil
- 1 tablespoon butter
- 10 garlic cloves, crushed
- 2 onions, sliced

- 1 bell pepper, sliced
- 2 teaspoons red chili pepper
- 1 teaspoon garam masala
- 1 teaspoon pepper powder
- 1 teaspoon vinegar
- ½ cup tomato ketchup
- Salt, to taste

DIRECTIONS

1. Preheat oil and butter in a pan. Add crushed garlic and cook for about 1 minute.
2. Add onions and salt. Cook until browned. Add sausage and cook for 8-10 minutes.
3. Add peppers and sauté for 2-3 minutes. Add chili powder and stir well.
4. Add ketchup and toss to coat. Add vinegar, garam masala powder and pepper powder, mix well to combine. Serve.

ZUCCHINI CHEESE AND GARLIC BREADSTICKS

Cooking time: 40 minutes - **Servings:** 2

INGREDIENTS:

- 4 zucchinis, grated
- ⅓ cup parmesan cheese, grated
- ⅓ cup cheddar cheese, grated
- ½ cup mozzarella cheese, grated
- 1 egg
- 1 tablespoon garlic powder
- 1 teaspoon pepper
- ½ teaspoon red pepper flakes
- ½ teaspoon salt

DIRECTIONS

1. Preheat the oven to 400°F.
2. Mix grated zucchini, parmesan cheese, garlic powder, pepper, red pepper flakes, salt, and egg in a bowl. Mix well to combine.
3. Line the baking sheet with parchment paper. Spread the mixture evenly on the baking sheet, about ½ inch thick.
4. Bake for 35-40 minutes. Top with cheddar and mozzarella cheese. Bake for 10 minutes more.
5. Let cool and slice into sticks. Serve.

SPINACH YOGURT CHEESE DIP WITH VEGGIES

Cooking time: 2 minutes - **Servings:** 8

INGREDIENTS:

- 2 cups fresh spinach
- 2 tablespoons Greek yogurt
- 3/4 cup cheddar cheese, shredded
- 1/4 cup parmesan cheese, shredded
- 1/4 teaspoon garlic powder
- 1/2 teaspoon salt

DIRECTIONS

1. Add spinach to a skillet and cook over medium heat for 2-3 minutes, stirring frequently.
2. Transfer to a plate and let cool slightly. Chop the spinach.
3. Mix cream cheese and Greek yogurt in a bowl. Add cheddar, parmesan, garlic powder and salt, stir well to combine.
4. Add spinach and stir well. Microwave the dip for 30 seconds and stir well. Serve with sliced veggies of choice.

ZUCCHINI MINI PIZZAS

Cooking time : 20 minutes - **Servings:** 24

INGREDIENTS:

- 1 zucchini, cut into 1/4 inch-slices
- 1/3 cup pizza sauce
- 3/4 cup mozzarella cheese, shredded
- 1/2 cup miniature pepperoni slices
- Minced fresh basil
- Salt, pepper, to taste

DIRECTIONS

1. Preheat broiler. Place zucchini slices in a single layer on a greased baking sheet.
2. Broil for 1-2 minutes per side.
3. Sprinkle zucchini with salt and pepper, top with sauce, cheese and pepperoni. Broil for about 1 minute. Serve topped with basil.

EGG SALAD IN LETTUCE CUPS

Cooking time: 2 minutes - **Servings:** 4

INGREDIENTS:

- 4 eggs, hard boiled, sliced
- 1 avocado, diced
- 8 leaves lettuce
- 2 teaspoons lemon juice
- 3 tablespoons mayonnaise
- 2 tablespoons chives, chopped
- 1/2 teaspoons salt
- 1/4 teaspoon pepper

DIRECTIONS

1. Mix lemon juice, mayonnaise, chives, salt and pepper in a bowl.
2. Mix eggs and avocado in a bowl. Top with the dressing and toss well to combine.
3. Add ¼ cup of the mixture into each lettuce leaf and serve.

GREEK SALAD WITH FETA

Cooking time : 2 minutes - **Servings:** 4

INGREDIENTS:

- 1 cucumber, sliced
- 2 bell peppers, sliced
- ½ red onion, sliced
- 4 oz Feta cheese, cubed
- 1/2 cup kalamata olives, pitted
- ¼ cup olive oil
- 1 tablespoon red wine vinegar
- 1 teaspoon dried oregano
- Salt, pepper, to taste

DIRECTIONS

1. Mix all the vegetables in a bowl. Add Feta cheese.
2. Add olives, drizzle with olive oil, vinegar, oregano, salt and pepper. Toss well to coat.
3. Serve right away.

JUGGAD WELE VEGETABLES

Cooking time: 20 minutes - **Servings:** 4

INGREDIENTS:

- 1 head broccoli, cut into florets
- 2 carrots, peeled and chopped
- 2 parsnips, peeled and chopped
- 1 teaspoon ground coriander
- 1 teaspoon turmeric
- 1 teaspoon curry powder
- 1 teaspoon cumin seeds
- 3 tablespoons olive oil
- 1 teaspoon grated ginger
- Sea salt, pepper, to taste

DIRECTIONS

1. Preheat the oven to 450 F.
2. Add all the vegetables to a bowl. Add coriander, turmeric, curry powder, cumin, salt and pepper, toss well to coat.
3. Add oil and toss to coat. Place the vegetables on a baking sheet in one layer. Bake for about 20 minutes. Toss with grated ginger and serve warm.

JHATPAT JHINGA

Cooking time: 20 minutes - **Servings:** 4

INGREDIENTS:

For Prawns:

- 1 lb prawns without shells
- 1/2 teaspoon turmeric powder
- 1 tablespoon oil
- 1/2 teaspoon salt

For the Gravy:

- 2 ½ cups onions finely chopped
- 2 ½ cups tomatoes finely chopped
- 2 tablespoons tomato paste
- 2 ½ teaspoons chili powder
- 1 teaspoon turmeric powder
- 1 tablespoon ginger garlic paste
- 6 tablespoons oil

- 3 ½ oz spring onions, for serving
- Fresh coriander, for serving
- Salt, taste

DIRECTIONS

1. Preheat oil in a pan over medium heat. Add prawns, salt, turmeric and cook for about 5 minutes. Remove from heat and set aside.
2. Preheat some oil in a separate pan over medium heat. Add onions and cook for about 3-4 minutes. Add ginger garlic paste, cook for 1 minute.
3. Add chili powder, turmeric powder and salt, cook for about 30 seconds.
4. Add tomatoes and cook for about 5 minutes. Add tomato paste to the gravy and cook for 1 minute.
5. Add prawns and cook for about 10 minutes. Add spring onions and coriander, stir well and serve.

FRITTATA WITH VEGETABLES

Cooking time: 30 minutes - **Servings:** 4

INGREDIENTS:

- 4 bacon slices, diced
- 1 cup mushrooms, sliced
- 2 tablespoons butter
- 4 oz baby spinach
- 1 cup Cheddar cheese, shredded
- 6 eggs
- 1/4 cup heavy cream
- Salt, pepper, to taste

DIRECTIONS

1. Preheat the oven to 355F. Preheat an oven proof pan over medium heat. Add bacon and cook for about 4 minutes. Add butter and mushrooms and cook for about 3 minutes.
2. Add spinach and cook for 2 minutes more. Remove from heat and sprinkle everything with cheese.
3. Mix eggs, cream, salt and pepper in a bowl. Pour the mixture to the pan and bake for 20 minutes.
4. Let rest for 5-10 minutes and serve.

MASALA FISH FRY

Cooking time: 40 minutes - **Servings :** 4

INGREDIENTS:

- 10 fish slices
- 1 tablespoon rice flour

- 10 dry red chillies
- 2 tablespoons coriander seeds
- 10 peppercorns
- 1 teaspoon cumin seeds
- 1 teaspoon fennel seeds
- 2 cloves
- 1 inch cinnamon stick
- 1 onion, chopped
- 2 curry leaves
- 5 garlic cloves
- 1/4 teaspoon turmeric powder
- 1 teaspoon lemon juice
- Salt, to taste
- Oil, for frying

DIRECTIONS

1. Toast roast the red chillies, coriander seeds, peppercorns, cumin seeds, fennel seeds, cloves and cinnamon stick until nice aroma comes out. Set aside.
2. Add few drops of oil to the same pan, add onions, curry leaves and garlic cloves, cook for 3-4 minutes.
3. Add roasted spices and onion-garlic to a jar, add turmeric powder, lemon juice and grind into a fine and thick paste with water.
4. Rub the thick paste evenly over the fish slices and let rest for at least two hours.
5. Fry the fish slices with enough oil over medium heat until browned on all sides. Serve.

CHINESE STYLE CHICKEN AND BROCCOLI STIR FRY

Cooking time: 15 minutes - **Servings :** 4

INGREDIENTS:

- 1 lb boneless skinless chicken breast, cut into bite sized pieces
- ¼ lb broccoli, cut into small florets
- 1 tablespoon olive oil
- 1/2 onion , minced
- 2 garlic cloves, minced
- 1 tablespoon fresh ginger, minced
- 1 tablespoon low sodium soy sauce
- 1 teaspoon sesame seed oil

- 2 teaspoons rice vinegar
- 2 teaspoons hot sauce

DIRECTIONS

1. Preheat oil in a skillet or a pan over medium heat. Add onions and garlic, cook for 3-4 minutes.
2. Add chicken and ginger, cook for 1 minute more.
3. Add soy sauce, sesame oil, rice wine vinegar and hot sauce. Cook for about 8-10 minutes, stirring from time to time.
4. Add broccoli and 1-2 tablespoons water. Cover the pan and cook for about 1-2 minutes. Serve.

PALAK PANEER

Cooking time: 30 minutes - **Servings : 4**

INGREDIENTS:

- 1 cup paneer, cubed
- 4 cups palak (or green spinach)
- 1 onion, chopped
- 1 teaspoon minced garlic
- ½ teaspoon minced ginger
- 1 teaspoon red chilli powder
- 1 teaspoon coriander powder
- ½ teaspoon cumin powder
- ¼ teaspoon turmeric powder
- A pinch kasuri methi
- 1 teaspoon garam masala
- 2 teaspoons ghee
- A pinch hing
- 1 teaspoon tomato paste
- 1 cup milk
- 1 tablespoon plain yogurt

DIRECTIONS

1. Bring a pot of water to a boil and add spinach leaves. Simmer for about 2 minutes and remove from heat. Add to a blender and puree to a smooth paste.
2. Preheat ghee in a pot. Add cumin powder and add the chopped onions. Sauté until golden brown and add coriander powder, turmeric, chilli powder and hing. Cook for a few seconds.
3. Add minced ginger and garlic and the tomato paste. Mix well and add the pureed spinach.
4. Add milk. Mix well, bring to boil and add the kasuri methi and salt.

5. Cook covered for about 6-8 minutes. Slowly add the paneer pieces, stir to coat.

6. Sprinkle with garam masala, mix well and remove from the heat.

7. Serve topped with yogurt.

MAST MASALA MUSSELS

Cooking time: 20 minutes - **Servings : 4**

INGREDIENTS:

- 4 lbs mussels, scrubbed
- 1 cup basil leaves, chopped
- 1/4 cup extra-virgin olive oil
- 1 onion, chopped
- 1 fennel bulb, trimmed and chopped
- 4 garlic cloves, chopped
- 1 teaspoon garam masala
- 1/4 teaspoon hot red-pepper flakes
- 1 can (15 oz) diced tomatoes with juices
- 2/3 cup canned unsweetened coconut milk

DIRECTIONS

1. Preheat oil in pot over medium-high heat. Add onion, fennel, garlic, garam masala, red-pepper flakes, salt and pepper, cook for about 10-12 minutes, stirring occasionally.

2. Add tomatoes with juices and coconut milk, bring everything to a boil. Add mussels and cover the pot. Cook for 8 - 10 minutes. Discard unopened mussels after 10 minutes.

3. Add basil, stir well and serve.

KETO CAULIFLOWER EGG FRIED RICE

Cooking time: 10 minutes - **Servings : 4**

INGREDIENTS:

- 12 oz cauliflower, riced
- 1 oz green onion, sliced
- 1/4 cup carrot, diced optional
- 2 tablespoons butter
- 2 garlic cloves, crushed
- 1 egg, beaten
- 2 tablespoons soy sauce
- 1 teaspoon toasted sesame oil

DIRECTIONS

1. Melt butter in a skillet over medium heat. Add carrots and cauliflower. Cook for about 5 minutes, stirring often.
2. Add green onions, cook for 2-3 minutes. Add garlic and cook for 1 minute more. Add egg and stir well to combine. Cook for 1-2 minutes, stirring frequently.
3. Add soy sauce and sesame oil. Serve.

SOYA PANEER CHEESE KABABS

Cooking time: 25 minutes - **Servings :** 6

INGREDIENTS:

- 1 cup soya granules, soaked in hot water for 10 mins, drained
- 1 cup paneer, grated
- 1 cup rice, pressed
- 2 onion, chopped
- 4 green chilli, chopped
- 1 tablespoon ginger paste
- 2 tablespoon chat masala
- 1 tablespoon coriander powder
- 1 tablespoon coriander leaves, chopped
- 1 tablespoon garlic paste
- 2 tablespoon garam masala powder
- 1 tablespoon chilli powder
- 2 cup mozzarella, grated
- 1 1/2 cup refined oil
- Salt, to taste

DIRECTIONS

1. Mix paneer, soya and the remaining ingredients in a bowl.
2. Divide the dough into smaller portions and shape them into kebabs and put onto a thick seekh.
3. Preheat oil in a deep pan over medium heat. Cook kebabs until browned on all sides. Serve.

PALAK METHI ROTI

Cooking time: 15 minutes - **Servings :** 4

INGREDIENTS:

- 1 cup blanched spinach, chopped
- 1/2 cup fenugreek (methi) leaves, chopped

- 2 cups coconut flour
- 1/2 cup paneer cheese, cubed
- 1 teaspoon ghee
- 1 onion , chopped
- 4 garlic cloves, grated
- 3 cardamoms
- 2 cloves
- ½ teaspoon garam masala
- Salt, to taste

DIRECTIONS

1. Preheat ghee in a pan over medium heat. Add cardamoms, cloves, onion and garlic. Cook for 3-4 minutes.
2. Add spinach, fenugreek leaves, paneer, garam masala and salt. Cook for 3-4 minutes, stirring often. Let cool slightly.
3. Mix flour and spinach mixture in a bowl. Slowly add water and knead the mixture into smooth dough.
4. Divide the dough into 8-10 portions of equal size. Roll each portion out into a flat paratha about 6-7 inches in diameter.
5. Preheat a skillet and place the rolled out paratha in the skillet, cook for 1-2 minutes per side. Serve.

MUSHROOM PEPPER MASALA

Cooking time: 30 minutes - **Servings :** 4

INGREDIENTS:

- 1 lb mushroom, chopped
- 1 onion, chopped
- 1 tomato, chopped
- 1 teaspoon ginger garlic paste
- 4 garlic cloves, crushed
- 1 green chilli, chopped
- 1 teaspoon coriander powder
- ½ teaspoon red chili powder
- ¼ teaspoon turmeric powder
- ¼ teaspoon garam masala
- 1 tablespoon olive oil
- ¼ teaspoon mustard seeds
- ¼ teaspoon cumin seeds

- ½ lemon, juiced
- Fresh cilantro, for serving
- Salt, to taste

DIRECTIONS

1. Preheat oil in a pan over medium heat. Add mustard seeds and cumin seeds, cook until soft.
2. Add onions, curry leaves and green chili, cook for 3-4 minutes. Add ginger garlic paste and chopped tomatoes.
3. Add turmeric powder, chili powder, coriander powder and garam masala. Cook for about 5-7 minutes.
4. Add mushrooms and cook it covered with little water, for about 5 minutes. Uncover and cook until all water evaporates.
5. Add lemon juice and stir well. Cook for 1 minute. Serve topped with cilantro.

BUTTER GARLIC PRAWNS

Cooking time: 18 minutes - **Servings : 4**

INGREDIENTS:

- 1 lb shrimp, peeled and deveined
- 6 tablespoons butter
- 5 garlic cloves, minced
- 1/2 cup chicken stock
- ¼ teaspoon red pepper flakes
- 2 tablespoons lemon juice
- 2 tablespoons parsley, minced
- Salt, pepper, to taste

DIRECTIONS

1. Preheat 2 tablespoons butter in a skillet over medium heat. Add shrimp, season with salt and pepper, cook for 4-5 minutes.
2. Transfer shrimp to a plate. Add garlic and cook for about 30 seconds.
3. Add chicken stock and stir well to combine. Cook for about 5-10 minutes.
4. Add the remaining butter, lemon juice and red pepper. Stir well and cook for 2 more minutes.
5. Add shrimp and stir to combine. Serve topped with parsley.

TANDOORI CHICKEN BOTI

Cooking time: 30 minutes - **Servings : 8**

INGREDIENTS:

- 8 chicken thighs

- 1/2 cup plain yogurt

- 2 tablespoons hot curry paste

- 1 tablespoon fish sauce

- 1 tablespoonlime juice

- 1/2 teaspoon stevia or splenda

DIRECTIONS

1. Combine all the marinade ingredients in a gallon sized ziploc bag and mix well.

2. Rinse and pat dry chicken thighs, and using a sharp knife, make a few deep cuts across the top of each thigh.

3. Put chicken into the ziploc bag, squeeze the excess air out and seal. Squeeze and squish the bag to make sure the chicken is well coated, then toss into the fridge. Marinate for at least 4 hours (overnight is even better).

4. Put chicken on a foil or parchment lined sheet pan.

5. Heat the oven to 450F and bake the chicken for about 40 minutes (longer if larger chicken thighs).

6. Once cooked, it is ready to serve.

SAAG MUTTON

Cooking time: 3 hours - **Servings : 2**

INGREDIENTS:

- 1 lb lamb stew meat, cubed

- 1 red onion, sliced

- 1 lb spinach

- 1 can (14 oz) diced tomatoes

- 2 garlic cloves

- 2 tablespoons ginger, minced

- 2 teaspoons ground cardamom

- 6 cloves

- 2 teaspoons ground coriander

- ½ teaspoon chili powder

- 1 teaspoon garam masala

- 2 teaspoons cumin

DIRECTIONS

1. Add all the ingredients except the spinach to a large pot, pour 1 cup water on top.

2. Bring everything to a boil, lower the heat to a simmer and cook covered for 2-3 hours.

3. Add spinach before serving, wilt it and serve.

GOBHI PARATHAS

Cooking time: 25 minutes - **Servings :** 12

INGREDIENTS:

- 3 cups coconut or almond flour
- 1 cup water
- 1 tablespoon ghee
- ½ cauliflower head, grated
- 1 green chili, chopped
- 1 teaspoon garam masala
- A pinch red chili powder
- Salt, to taste

DIRECTIONS

1. Mix flour, salt and ghee in a bowl. Add water and knead until smooth dough is formed. Cover and refrigerate for 20-30 minutes.
2. Mix cauliflower and green chili in a separate bowl. Stir well to combine.
3. Now shape 2 medium sized balls from the dough. Dust with more flour. Roll both balls out to 3-4 inches circle.
4. Spread some ghee on top of each circle, top with cauliflower mixture, garam masala, red chili and salt. Press and seal the edges.
5. Dust the paratha with four and gently roll out to a size of a roti.
6. Preheat ghee in a skillet over medium heat. Add parathas and cook until browned on all sides. Serve.

KERALA STYLE EGG CURRY

Cooking time: 30 minutes - **Servings :** 4

INGREDIENTS:

- 4 eggs, hard boiled, halved
- 1 onion, sliced
- 3 green chilies, chopped
- 1 tomato, chopped
- 1 ½ cups coconut milk, medium thick
- ¾ cup thick coconut milk
- 2 sprigs curry leaves
- ¼ teaspoon mustard seeds
- 1 ½ teaspoons garlic paste

- 1 ½ teaspoons ginger paste
- ¼ teaspoon turmeric powder
- 1 tablespoon kashmiri chili powder
- 1 ½ teaspoons garam masala
- ½ teaspoon fennel powder
- 1 teaspoon pepper powder
- 1 tablespoon coriander powder
- Vegetable oil
- Salt, to taste

DIRECTIONS

1. Preheat oil in a skillet over medium heat. Add mustard seeds, onion, green chili, curry leaves and salt. Cook for about 5 minutes.
2. Add ginger and garlic paste, sauté for 1-2 minutes.
3. Add turmeric powder, chilli powder, pepper powder, coriander powder, garam masala and fennel powder. Cook for 3-4 minutes.
4. Add tomato, sauté for 2-3 minutes more. Add medium thick coconut milk and salt. Mix well to combine.
5. Add eggs and cook for 10 minutes coating the eggs. Add thick coconut milk and stir well until combined. Serve.

ROASTED LEMONY GARLICKY BROCCOLI

Cooking time: 20 minutes - **Servings :** 8

INGREDIENTS:

- 2 heads broccoli, broken into florets
- 2 tablespoons olive oil
- 2 teaspoons salt
- 6 garlic cloves, minced
- 1/2 lemon, juiced

DIRECTIONS

1. Preheat oven to 400 F.
2. Toss all the ingredients in a bowl. Spread out the broccoli florets ona baking tray lined with parchment paper.
3. Bake for 15-20 minutes and serve.

CUCUMBER PEANUT SALAD

Cooking time: 10 minutes - **Servings** : 4

INGREDIENTS:

- 2 cucumber, sliced
- ½ cup fresh cilantro, chopped
- ¼ cup roasted sesame seeds
- 2 tablespoons fresh lime juice
- 1 ½ tablespoons fish sauce
- 1 tablespoon coconut aminos
- 1 tablespoon apple cider vinegar
- 1 garlic clove, minced
- 1/4 teaspoon red pepper flakes
- 2 teaspoons sesame oil
- Salt, pepper, to taste

DIRECTIONS

1. Mix lime juice, fish sauce, coconut aminos, vinegar, garlic, chilies or pepper flakes, sesame oil, salt and pepper in a bowl.
2. In a separate bowl, mix cucumber, cilantro and sesame seeds. Add dressing and toss to coat. Serve.

GUACAMOLE

Cooking time: 10 minutes - **Servings** : 4

INGREDIENTS:

- 1 avocado
- 2 teaspoons lime juice
- 1/4 teaspoon ground cumin
- 1 garlic clove, crushed
- 1/8 teaspoon chilli powder
- 1/8 teaspoon smoked paprika
- 1 tablespoon cilantro, chopped
- 2 tablespoons scallions, sliced
- 1 tablespoon sour cream
- ¼ teaspoon salt
- A pinch pepper

DIRECTIONS

1. Scoop the avocado flesh into a bowl and add lime juice.
2. Mash the avocado with a fork and add the remaining ingredients and mix well. Serve.

MILLIE AUR JULIE WALI SABJI

Cooking time: 40 minutes - **Servings** : 4

INGREDIENTS:

- 2 onion, chopped
- ¼ cup coconut
- 1 cup carrots, diced
- ¼ cup cauliflower florets
- ¼ cup beans, chopped
- 2 oz paneer, cubed
- 2 tablespoons oil
- ½ teaspoon cumin seeds
- ¼ teaspoon asafetida
- 4 curry leaves
- 2 green chillies
- 3 dry red chillies
- 2 bay leaves
- ½ tablespoon ginger garlic paste
- 6 tomatoes, blended
- 1 teaspoon red chili powder
- ¼ teaspoon black pepper
- 1 teaspoon amchoor powder
- 1 teaspoon garam masala
- 1 teaspoon sambhar masala
- ¼ teaspoon sugar
- A handful coriander, chopped
- ½ teaspoon corn flour
- ¼ cup bell pepper, diced
- 2 tablespoons coconut milk
- Salt, black pepper, to taste

DIRECTIONS

1. Preheat oil in a skillet over medium heat. Add cauliflower and carrots, fry for 3-4 minutes. Add beans and cook for 1-2 minutes more. Remove to a plate.
2. Add paneer and cook until browned on all sides.
3. Ina separate skillet, preheat oil too. Add onion and cook for 3-4 minutes. Add coconut and cook for 1-2 minutes more. Transfer to a blender and puree until smooth.

4. Add more oil to the pan. Add cumin seeds, asafetida, curry leaves, green chillies and dry red chillies. Also add bay leaves and stir well. Add garlic paste, stir again, cook for 30 seconds.

5. Add onion and coconut paste and cook for 1-2 minutes. Add tomato paste, season with salt and bring to a boil.

6. Add masalas to the mixture and stir well. Add the vegetables and beans mixture, add paneer and the remaining ingredients. Cook for 5-10 minutes over low heat. Serve.

CHEESE AND CREAM SPINACH

Cooking time: 10 minutes - **Servings :** 4

INGREDIENTS:

- 3 tablespoons butter
- 4 garlic cloves, minced
- 10 oz baby spinach, chopped
- ½ cup heavy cream
- 3 oz cream cheese
- 1 teaspoon Italian seasoning
- ¼ teaspoon sea salt
- ¼ teaspoon black pepper

DIRECTIONS

1. Preheat butter in a pan over medium heat. Add minced garlic and cook until fragrant.

2. Add spinach. Cook for 2-4 minutes, until wilted.

3. Add heavy cream, cream cheese, sea salt, black pepper and Italian seasoning. Cook until cream cheese melts, stirring constantly. Keep cooking until cheese thickens. Serve.

KESAR KALAKAND

Cooking time: 15 minutes - **Servings :** 24

INGREDIENTS:

- 2 ½ cups packed Paneer, grated
- 1 can (14 oz) condensed milk
- 4 tablespoons milk powder
- ½ teaspoon cardamom powder
- 3 tablespoons nuts of choice, chopped
- A pinch saffron strands
- 1 tablespoon dried rose petals, for serving

DIRECTIONS

1. Mix about 2 tablespoons warm milk with saffron and let ewst.

2. Prepare a baking pan and line with parchment paper.

3. Mix paneer, condensed milk, milk powder and cardamom in a pan. Place over medium heat, cook until the mixture loosens in the heat.

4. Reduce the heat to low and cook for 15 minutes, stirring frequently.

5. Pour the mixture into the prepared baking pan, smooth well with a spoon.

6. Drizzle the saffron and some of the milk on top. Top with chopped nuts and rose petals.

7. Let cool and cover, refrigerate for at least 2 hours.

8. Cut into pieces and serve.

ALMOND WALNUT CHOCOLATE MOUSSE

Cooking time: 5 minutes - **Servings :** 4

INGREDIENTS:

- flesh of 2 ripe avocados
- ¼ cup regular cocoa powder
- ¼ cup melted chocolate chips
- 3 tablespoons almond milk
- ½ teaspoon pure vanilla extract
- ¼ cup maple syrup
- ¼ cup almonds and walnuts mix, chopped

DIRECTIONS

1. Combine all ingredients except for nuts in a blender or food processor until completely smooth.

2. Fold in nuts and stir well to combine. Cover and refrigerate for at least 2 hours. Serve.

COCONUT AND CREAM BARFI

Cooking time: 15 minutes - **Servings :** 12

INGREDIENTS:

- 3 cups coconut, grated
- 1 ½ cups sugar
- 3/4 cup heavy whipping cream
- 3 tablespoons confectioner's sugar
- 1/2 teaspoon freshly ground cardamom
- Ghee, for greasing
- Pistachios, chopped, for serving

DIRECTIONS

1. Preheat a non-stick kadhai over medium heat and add grated coconut, sugar and cream. Mix well till well combined.
2. Cook until the mixture is golden, stirring all the time.
3. Remove from heat and add cardamom powder and confectioners' sugar, stir well.
4. Grease a pan with ghee, pour the mixture into the pan. Sprinkle with nuts and let rest for at least 1 hour in the fridge, Cut into pieces and serve.

KETO ROCKY ROAD

Cooking time: 5 minutes - **Servings :** 2
INGREDIENTS:

- 1 cup grass-fed butter
- 2 cups marshmallows
- 2 cups hazelnuts
- ¼ cup almonds
- ¼ cup freeze dried blueberries
- 14 oz dark chocolate chips

DIRECTIONS

1. Add hazelnuts and almonds to a dry skillet and toast for about 5 minutes over medium heat.
2. Line a baking sheet with parchment paper. Melt chocolate chips and butter in a bowl, stir well until smooth. Let cool to room temperature.
3. Add nuts, marshmallows and blueberries to the batter and pour into the baking sheet. Cover and refrigerate for at least 2-3 hours.
4. Cut into pieces and serve.

CHOCOLATE AND COFFEE ICE CREAM

Cooking time: 15 minutes - **Servings :** 2
INGREDIENTS:

- 1 ¾ cups heavy whipping cream
- 1/2 unsweetened almond milk
- 1 ½ teaspoons instant coffee
- 3 egg yolks
- 2 oz sugar free dark chocolate, chopped
- ½ teaspoon vanilla extract
- ¼ teaspoon xanthan gum
- 2 tablespoons sweetener of choice

DIRECTIONS

1. Mix cream, almond milk, sweetener and coffee in a saucepan over medium heat. Stir until sweetener and coffee dissolve.
2. Whisk the egg yolks in a bowl. Slowly add the hot cream mixture, whisking continuously. Pour the mixture to the pan and cook for 3-4 minutes, stirring constantly.
3. Let cool for about 20 minutes. Wrap tightly in plastic wrap and chill for at least 3 hours.
4. Add vanilla extract. Sprinkle with the xanthan gum and whisk vigorously to combine. Pour the mixture into an ice cream maker and process as per the manufacturer's directions.
5. Add the chopped chocolate. Transfer the mixture to an airtight container and freeze until firm.

KETO MACAROON

Cook time : 8 minutes - **Servings :** 10

INGREDIENTS:

*   ¼ cup almond flour
*   ½ cup shredded coconut
*   2 tablespoons Swerve
*   1 tablespoon vanilla extract
*   1 tablespoon coconut oil
*   3 egg whites

DIRECTIONS

1. Preheat the oven to 400F.
2. Mix almond flour, coconut and swerve in a bowl.
3. Add coconut oil to a sauce pan and melt over low heat. Add vanilla, stir to combine.
4. Whisk egg whites until stiff peaks form. Slowly add egg whites to the flour mixture, mix well to incorporate.
5. Pour the mixture into the muffin cups and bake for 8 minutes. Let cool before serving.

SHRIKHAND

Cook time: 10 minutes + chilling time - **Servings:** 2

INGREDIENTS:

*   3/4 cup Greek yogurt
*   2 tablespoons Erythritol
*   few strands saffron crushed into mortar and pestle
*   1 teaspoon milk
*   1/4 teaspoon green cardamom seeds powder

- 4-5 cashew nuts chopped finely
- 4-5 almonds chopped finely
- 4-5 pistachios chopped finely, optional

DIRECTIONS

1. Dissolve crushed saffron in the warm milk.
2. Put Greek yogurt, Erythritol into a bowl and stir till everything is combined well.
3. Add saffron milk, cardamom powder, chopped nuts and mix well.
4. Put it into a refrigerator for couple of hours before serving.

BADAM KULFI

Cook time: 4 hours 20 minutes - **Servings:** 4

INGREDIENTS:

- 2 cups ground almonds, blanched & peeled
- 2 cups condensed milk
- 1/2 cup milk
- 8 tablespoons fresh cream
- 15 strand saffron
- 6 pieces pistachios
- 2 tablespoons blanched almonds

DIRECTIONS

1. Combine ground almonds, cream condensed milk in a large bowl and whisk until thick. Set aside.
2. Heat milk in a saucepan on a high flame and then boil it.
3. When milk starts boiling, add saffron strands and mix well. Then remove pan from the flame and let the mixture cool.
4. Once it cools, combine it with the almond mixture and stir well (the consistency should be creamy and thick).
5. Heat another pan on a moderate flame, add coarsely chopped pistachios, almonds and dry roast for a few seconds.
6. Once done, combine it with the kulfi mixture (reserve some for garnish), mix well and pour the mixture into the kulfi moulds.
7. Cover the top with a lid and keep in a freezer for 4 hours or until set.
8. Once done, remove kulfi from the mould and sprinkle with some of the reserved pistachios and almonds.

LAUKI KI KHEER

Cook time: 40 minutes - **Servings :** 6

INGREDIENTS:

- 2 tablespoons ghee
- 12 almonds, crushed
- 12 cashews, crushed
- 2 cups Lauki/Bottle gourd, grated
- 12 strands Saffron
- 2 tablespoons sweetener of choice
- 1 teaspoon Cardamom powder

DIRECTIONS

1. Preheat ghee in a pan over medium heat. Add almonds and cashews and fry until browned.
2. Add grated Lauki and fry for 5-6 minutes on low heat.
3. Add milk and bring everything to a boil. Reduce the heat to low and cook until the mixture thickens.
4. Add saffron and cook on low heat for 20-25 minutes, stirring from time to time.
5. Add cardamom powder and sweetener, cook for 3-4 minutes.
6. Serve topped with almond and pistachio slivers and rose petals. Serve chilled.

MUG MAIN MASTI

Cook time: 40 minutes - **Servings :** 6

INGREDIENTS:

- 2 tablespoons unsalted grass-fed butter
- 1 1/2 tablespoons cocoa powder
- 2 tablespoons erythritol
- 1 egg
- 2 tablespoons almond flour
- 1 tablespoon golden flaxseed meal
- 2 teaspoons coconut flour
- 1/2 teaspoon baking powder
- A pinch of salt

DIRECTIONS

1. Melt butter in a bowl. Add cocoa and sweetener, mix until well combined.
2. Add egg and mix until smooth. Add the remaining ingredients and pour the batter into a mug.
3. Place a paper towel into the microwave and place the mug on top. Cook on high for 70-90 seconds. Let cool for a couple minutes and enjoy!

CHICKPEA SUNDAL

Servings: 10

INGREDIENTS

- 2 tablespoons virgin coconut oil or vegetable oil
- 12 fresh curry leaves
- 6 dried kashmiri or guajillo chiles, broken into pieces, seeds removed
- 1 1/2 tablespoons black or brown mustard seeds
- 1/2 teaspoon asafetida (optional)
- 1/4 pound 15- can chickpeas, rinsed
- kosher salt
- 1/2 cup freshly grated coconut or unsweetened shredded coconut
- lime wedges (for serving)
- asafetida is a combination of dried gum resins from plant roots; available at indian markets.

DIRECTIONS

1. Warmth oil in a huge skillet over medium-high. Make mustard seeds, swirling pan sometimes until oil starts to sputter. Add curry leaves, chiles, and asafetida (if using) and prepare, stirring sometimes, until curry leaves are somewhat darkened about 45 mere seconds. Add chickpeas; make, tossing often, simply until warmed through, about three minutes. Let cool; time of year with salt.
2. Scoop Sunday right into a bowl; beat with coconut. Serve with lime wedges.

SLOW-COOKER CHICKEN TIKKA MASALA

Servings: 10

INGREDIENTS

- 2/3 cup plain greek yogurt
- 1 teaspoon ground coriander (optional)
- 4 pounds . boneless skinless chicken breasts, cut into 1" cubes
- kosher salt
- freshly ground black pepper
- 2 onions, chopped
- 2/3 cup garlic, minced
- 2 tablespoons freshly minced ginger
- 1 teaspoon ground turmeric
- 1 1/2 tablespoons ground cumin
- 1 1/2 tablespoons paprika
- 1 1/2 tablespoons garam masala

- 1 teaspoon cayenne pepper
- 2 cans 1 (28-oz.) crushed tomatoes
- 1 cup heavy cream
- kosher salt
- freshly chopped cilantro, for garnish
- rice or naan, for serving

DIRECTIONS

1. In the plate of the slow cooker, combine chicken, yogurt, and coriander; period with salt and pepper. Let marinate a quarter-hour. Mix in onion, garlic, ginger, and spices, after that add tomatoes. Cover and make until chicken is prepared through, on high for 4 hours or on low for 8 hours. Mix in cream and garnish with cilantro before serving.

SUSAN FENIGER

Servings: 10

INGREDIENTS

- 1/2 cup vegetable oil
- 2 1/2 pounds white onions, chopped
- 6 serrano chiles, sliced into rounds
- 2 2-inch-long piece fresh ginger, peeled, thinly sliced
- 8 garlic cloves, chopped
- 20 whole cloves
- 2 tablespoons cumin seeds
- 2 tablespoons ground cinnamon
- 1 1/2 tablespoons ground cardamom
- 2 teaspoons black peppercorns
- 15 cups (60 ounces) plain whole-milk yogurt, divided
- 3/4 cup fresh lemon juice
- 2 whole lamb shoulder (about 10 pounds), boned, trimmed of all fat (about 4 1/3 pounds)
- 3 tablespoons coarse kosher salt, divided
- 4 cups sliced almonds (about 7 ounces)
- 2 cups raw cashews (about 5 ounces)
- 1 cup (packed) golden brown sugar
- 2 tablespoons coarse kosher salt

DIRECTIONS

1. Heat oil in a large skillet over medium-high warmth. Add onions; sauté until golden, 14 moments. Add

garlic and then 7 ingredients; stir 2 minutes. Scrape combination into the processor. Add 4 cups yogurt. Mix until mixture is usually coarse puree; transfer to a large bowl. Mix in 2 cups yogurt and lemon juice.

2. Place 1 glass yogurt marinade in normal size bowl. Cover, chill, and reserve for topping. Place 3 cups marinade in moderate bowl; mix in staying 1 1/2 cups yogurt and time of year with salt and pepper. Cover, chill, and reserve for sauce.

3. Place lamb in a large roasting pan and form into a rectangle approximately 12x6 ins (some slim layers may overlap). Sprinkle with 2 1/4 teaspoons salt; pass on with fifty percent of remaining marinade. Cautiously change lamb over. Sprinkle with staying 2 1/4 teaspoons salt; pass on with staying marinade. Cover with plastic material wrap. Refrigerate overnight.

4. Preheat oven to 375°F. Mix almonds, cashews, sugar, salt, and 1 glass marinade reserved for topping in processor chip until nuts are coarsely cut.

5. Remove plastic material and scrape the majority of the marinade off the best of lamb. Cover pan with foil and roast lamb for 1 1/2 hours. Uncover; pass on nut topping equally over. Roast lamb uncovered until topping is usually golden and lamb is usually tender about one hour. Let stand for ten minutes.

6. Transfer lamb to a platter. Serve, moving reserved sauce.

TELANGANA CHICKEN (TELANGANA-STYLE CURRIED CHICKEN STEW)

Servings: 4

INGREDIENTS

- 3 cups coconut milk
- 10 tbsp. plain, full-fat yogurt
- 2 tbsp. garam masala
- 2 teaspoons red chile powder, preferably kashmiri, or cayenne
- 3/4 cup garlic, peeled
- 6 tbsp. fresh lime juice
- 2 pieces 1 (4") ginger, peeled and thinly sliced
- kosher salt, to taste
- 6 pounds . chicken drumsticks and thighs, skin removed
- 54 fresh or frozen curry leaves, defrosted if frozen
- 16 green cardamom pods
- 2 pieces mace (optional)
- 2 star anise
- 1 cup cinnamon

- 1/2 cup canola or peanut oil
- 6 small green thai chiles or 1 1/2 serranos, halved
- 4 medium yellow onions, halved and thinly sliced crosswise
- 2 tbsp. chopped cilantro

DIRECTIONS

1. Purée coconut milk, yogurt, lime juice, garam masala, chile powder, garlic, ginger, and salt in a meals processor until clean; transfer to a bowl. Add poultry, 20 curry leaves, the cardamom, mace, if using, the celebrity anise, and cinnamon; toss to mix. Cover with plastic material wrap and chill overnight.

2. The very next day, heat oil within an 8-qt. saucepan over medium-high. Make chiles and onions until caramelized, about 20 minutes. Utilizing a slotted spoon, transfer combination to a bowl; reserve. Add poultry and its own marinade to pan; boil. Reduce heat to moderate; simmer until poultry is cooked through, about thirty minutes. Mix in chiles and onions; cook five minutes even more and garnish with cilantro and staying curry leaves.

SARA DICKERMAN

Servings: 10

INGREDIENTS

- 1/4 cup coconut or canola oil
- 2 teaspoons cumin seeds
- 6 garlic cloves, chopped
- 2 tablespoons finely chopped fresh ginger
- 2 teaspoons mustard seeds
- 2 medium onions, chopped
- fine sea salt
- 2 teaspoons ground turmeric
- pinch of cayenne pepper
- 4 large tomatoes, grated on a large grate, with juices reserved
- 2 1/2 pounds eggplant, cut into 1/2-inch cubes (about 5 cups)
- 2 ounces 15- can chickpeas, drained, rinsed, or 1 1/4 cups drained cooked chickpeas
- 2 1/2 tablespoons finely chopped jalapeño
- 2 shallots, finely chopped
- 2 tablespoons fresh lime juice, plus more
- 2 teaspoons honey
- 1/4 cup unsweetened flaked coconut
- 2 cups coarsely chopped mint leaves

- 1/2 cup coarsely chopped cilantro leaves
- freshly ground black pepper
- plain yogurt (for serving)

DIRECTIONS

1. Heat oil more than medium-high in a sizable skillet or Dutch oven. Add cumin and mustard seeds and prepare for 30 seconds, after that add garlic and ginger. Stir continuously until garlic just starts to brown, about 1 minute, then mix in onion and a generous pinch of salt. Cook, stirring often, until onion is normally tender, about five minutes. Mix in turmeric and cayenne. Pour in tomatoes and their juices, scraping up any browned bits with a wooden spoon. Add eggplant, chickpeas, ¼ cup drinking water, and a pinch of salt, mix and reduce high temperature to medium-low. Cover the pan and simmer until eggplant is normally tender, about a quarter-hour.
2. Remove from high temperature and increase jalapeño, shallot, lime juice, and honey. Fold in coconut, mint, and cilantro. Season to flavor with salt, dark pepper, and lime juice.
3. Best with a dollop of yogurt before serving.

ALAINA SULLIVAN

Servings: 10

INGREDIENTS

- 2 cups whole milk or unsweetened nut milk (such as hemp, almond, or cashew)
- 1 teaspoon ground turmeric
- 1/2 teaspoon ground ashwagandha (or another adaptogen, like shatavari or astralagus)
- 1 teaspoon ground cinnamon
- 1/4 teaspoon of ground cardamom
- pinch of ground ginger (optional)
- pinch of ground nutmeg
- freshly ground black pepper
- 2 teaspoons virgin coconut oils or ghee
- 2 teaspoons honey, preferably raw

DIRECTIONS

1. Bring milk to a simmer in a little saucepan over medium-low high temperature. Whisk in cinnamon, turmeric, ashwagandha, cardamom, ginger, if using, and nutmeg; period with pepper. Whisk vigorously to include any clumps. Add coconut essential oil, reduce high temperature to low, and continue steadily to make until warmed through, 5-10 minutes (the much longer you move, the more powerful the medication). Remove from high temperature and let cool somewhat. Stir in honey (you wish to avoid cooking food honey or you'll destroy its curing goodness). Pour right into a mug, beverage warm, and climb directly into bed.

SPICE-MARINATED AND GRILLED LAMB CHOPS

Servings: 10

INGREDIENTS

- 1 teaspoon fennel seeds
- 2 2-inch piece ginger, peeled, finely grated
- 8 garlic cloves, finely grated
- 1/2 cup crème fraîche or sour cream
- 2 serrano chile, finely grated
- 1/4 cup fresh lime juice
- 2 tablespoons mustard oils (optional)
- 2 teaspoons dried mangos powder (amchoor; optional)
- 2 teaspoons dried fenugreek leaves
- 2 teaspoons freshly ground black pepper
- 1 teaspoon finely grated nutmeg
- 2 teaspoons kashmiri chili powder or paprika, plus more for serving
- 1/4 cup vegetable oil, plus more for grill
- 24 lamb rib chops (about 2 1/4 pounds total), frenched
- kosher salt
- leaf mint , cilantro leaves with tender stems, and lemons wedges (for serving)
- a spice mill or mortar and pestle

DIRECTIONS

1. Toast fennel seeds in a dried-out small skillet over moderate heat, shaking pan frequently, until fragrant, about 45 seconds; let great. Finely grind in a spice mill or with mortar and pestle. Transfer to a sizable bowl; add chile, ginger, garlic, crème fraîche, lime juice, mustard essential oil (if using), mango powder (if using), fenugreek leaves, pepper, nutmeg, 1 tsp. chili powder, and 2 Tbsp. vegetable essential oil and mix well. Period lamb chops with salt and increases marinade; turn to layer. Cover and chill for at least 2 hours.

2. Allow lamb chops to sit at area temperature one hour before grilling.

3. Make a grill for moderate heat; essential oil grate. Grill lamb to preferred doneness, about three minutes per aspect for medium-uncommon. Transfer to a platter; let rest 5-10 minutes.

4. Best lamb with mint and cilantro and dust with an increase of chili powder. Serve with lemon wedges.

5. Do Ahead: Lamb could be marinated 12 hours forward. Keep chilled.

ALISON ROMAN

Servings: 10

INGREDIENTS

- 1 1/2 cups whole milk
- 2 ounces 1/4- envelope active dry yeast
- 7 cups all-purpose flour plus more for surface and hands
- 2 teaspoons kosher salt plus more
- 2 teaspoons sugar
- 2 small onions, finely chopped
- 2 cups whole-milk yogurt (not greek)
- 1/4 cup melted ghee (clarified butter) or vegetable oil plus more

DIRECTIONS

1. Heat milk in a little saucepan over medium-low warmth until an instant-read thermometer registers 100°. Transfer to a little bowl and whisk in yeast and sugars. Allow standing until foamy, about ten minutes.

2. Whisk 3 1/2 cups flour and 1 teaspoon salt in a huge bowl to mix. Add yeast combination, onion, yogurt, and 2 tablespoons ghee. Blend dough until blended but nonetheless shaggy.

3. Transfer dough to a lightly floured function surface area. Knead until an easy dough forms, adding flour as required (dough will become sticky), about five minutes. Gently grease another large bowl with ghee, place dough in the bowl, and change to coating. Cover with plastic material wrap. Allow rise in a warm, draft-free region until doubled in proportions, about 1 hour.

4. Punch straight down dough and divide it into 10 items. Using floured hands, roll each piece right into a ball on a gently floured surface area. Cover with plastic material wrap; let rest ten minutes.

5. Heat a huge cast-iron or another heavy skillet over medium-high warmth. Lightly coating with ghee. Dealing with 1 piece at the same time, stretch dough together with your hands or roll out with a rolling pin to 1/8-in. thickness. Sprinkle with salt. Cook until gently blistered, puffed, and prepared through, about 2 minutes per part. Wrap in foil to maintain warm until prepared to serve.

6. Perform AHEAD: Naan dough could be produced 4 hours before shaping. Cover and chill.

SANDESH (BENGALI MILK SWEETS)

Servings: 4

INGREDIENTS

- 2 1/2 tablespoons fresh lemon juice
- 2 1/2 tablespoons sugar
- 4 cups whole milk

- 1/2 teaspoon ground cardamom
- golden raisins or shelled pistachios, for garnish

DIRECTIONS

1. Bring milk to a boil in a 6-qt. saucepan, stirring occasionally to avoid scorching. Add lemon juice and remove from temperature; large curds will form. Utilizing a wooden spoon, lightly push curds collectively toward one part of the pot; usually do not mix or the curd will break right into small pieces. Range a fine-mesh sieve with dampened cheesecloth; stress curds and discard whey or conserve for another make use of. Rinse curds under cool running water.

2. Gather edges of cheesecloth together to create a purse. Tie edges around a wooden spoon. Place the spoon over a huge pot, balancing ends of a spoon to ensure that purse hangs openly. Let drain at space temperature for one hour; discard any liquid that collects in the pot. Transfer purse to a colander and cover with a heavy-bottom pot filled up with drinking water; allow cheese drain one hour.

3. Unwrap cheese and transfer to a function surface area. Using hands, knead cheese until soft ball forms, 2-3 minutes. Steadily add sugar and cardamom; knead until smooth. Temperature a 12" nonstick skillet over medium. Make cheese mixture, stirring sometimes, until slightly dry, however, not golden, about ten minutes. Remove from temperature and let cool somewhat. Using hands, divide the dough into 8 balls. Press a golden raisin or pistachio into each ball.

ALOO AUR GOSHT KA KALIYA (HYDERABADI-STYLE LAMB WITH POTATOES)

Servings: 8

INGREDIENTS

- 2/3 cup olive oil
- 12 green cardamom pods
- 12 whole cloves
- 2 pounds . medium red potatoes, peeled and quartered
- 6 medium onions, halved and thinly sliced crosswise
- 4 pounds . bone-in lamb shoulder, cut into 2" pieces (ask your butcher)
- kosher salt, to taste
- 2 teaspoons red chile powder, preferably kashmiri, or cayenne
- 1 1/2 teaspoons ground turmeric
- 1/4 cup garlic, mashed into a paste
- 2 pieces 1 (1") ginger, peeled and grated

- 2 cups plain, full-fat yogurt
- 1 1/2 cups minced cilantro
- 2 tbsp. pumpkins seeds, ground in a spice grinder
- 6 small green thai chiles, or 1 serrano, halved
- 1 teaspoon garam masala

DIRECTIONS

1. Heat oil in an 8-qt. saucepan over medium-high. Produce potatoes until golden, 10-12 minutes; employing a slotted spoon, transfer to a bowl. Add cardamom and cloves to pan; cook until fragrant, about 1 minute. Add onions; cook until relatively caramelized, about 20 occasions. Transfer onions to bowl with potatoes. Season lamb with salt; make, turning simply because required, until browned, 8-10 occasions. Add chile powder, turmeric, garlic, and ginger; make 1 minute. Add yogurt 1/4 glass simultaneously and stirring occasionally until lamb mixture is thick and relatively dry, 10-12 occasions. Add 2 cups normal water; boil. Reduce warmth to medium-low; make, protected, until lamb is certainly tender, about 1 hour. Mix in reserved potatoes and onions, the cilantro, flooring pumpkin seeds, chiles, and salt. Mix softly to mix and offer to a simmer once more. Simmer until potatoes are tender, about quarter-hour a lot more. Mix in garam masala before serving.

SOUTH INDIAN CURRY-MASHED POTATOES (ALOO MASALA)

Servings: 8

Ingredient

- 4 pounds . yukon gold potatoes
- 1/2 cup canola oil
- 1 teaspoon asafoetida
- 1 teaspoon fenugreek seeds
- 2 teaspoons black mustard seeds
- 40 fresh or frozen curry leaves
- 1/2 cup garlic, chopped
- 6 small green thai chiles or 1 serrano, halved
- 2 large yellow onions, roughly chopped
- 1 cup frozen peas
- 3 tbsp. ground coriander
- 2 teaspoons ground turmeric
- 2 (2-inch) piece ginger, peeled and grated
- kosher salt, to taste

- 2/3 cup chopped cilantro

DIRECTIONS

1. Make potatoes in boiling drinking water until just tender, 25-30 a few minutes; drain, peel, and trim into 2" pieces. High-temperature oil in a 6-qt. saucepan over medium-high. Make mustard seeds until they pop, 1-2 a few minutes. Add asafoetida, fenugreek seeds, and curry leaves; make 1 minute. Add garlic, chiles, and onion; prepare until golden, 8-10 a few minutes. Add potatoes, peas, coriander, turmeric, ginger, salt, and 1/2 glass water; boil. Reduce high temperature to medium-low; cook, protected, until potatoes are tender, 8-10 a few minutes. Uncover and mix, mashing gently; cook until slightly dried out, 4-5 minutes. Mix in cilantro.

SAMOSAS (FRIED POTATO-FILLED PASTRIES)

Servings: 12

INGREDIENTS

- 1 1/2 cups flour
- 4 tbsp. unsalted butter, cubed and chilled
- kosher salt, to taste
- 1/4 pound . russet potatoes, peeled and roughly chopped
- 1 carrot, roughly chopped
- 6 tablespoons ice-cold water
- 1 tbsp. canola oil, plus more
- 1/2 teaspoon cumin seeds
- 1/2 small yellow onion, minced
- 6 tablespoons frozen peas, defrosted
- 2 tablespoons minced cilantro
- 2 tablespoons minced mint
- 1/4 teaspoon garam masala
- 1 small green thai chiles or 1 serrano, minced
- 1/2 piece 1 (1") of ginger, peeled and minced
- tamarind and coconut-cilantro chutneys, for serving (optional)

DIRECTIONS

1. Make the dough: Pulse flour, butter, and salt in a food processor chip into pea-size crumbles. Add drinking water; pulse until dough forms. Divide into 12 balls; chill one hour.
2. Make the filling: Boil potatoes and carrots in a 4-qt. a saucepan of salted drinking water until tender, 8-10 a few minutes. Drain; coarsely mash. Add 2 tbsp. essential oil to pan; high temperature over

medium-high. Make cumin seeds until they pop, 1-2 a few minutes. Add onion and ginger; cook until golden, 4-6 minutes. Let great; stir into potato mix with peas, cilantro, mint, garam masala, chiles, and salt.

3. Type and fry samosas: Dealing with 1 ball at the same time, roll the dough right into a 6" circular; cut in two. Gather direct edges of just one 1 half-round jointly, overlapping by 1/4" to create a cone. Moisten seam with drinking water; press to seal. Spoon 1 tbsp. filling into cone. Moisten edges of a cone with drinking water; pinch to seal. High temperature 2" essential oil in a 6-qt. saucepan until a deep-fry thermometer reads 350°. Fry samosas until sharp, 8-10 minutes. Drain in some recoverable format towels; serve with chutneys if you want.

ALOO GOBI

Servings: 10
INGREDIENTS

- 1/4 cup vegetable oil
- 2 red chili, diced
- 2 tablespoons minced ginger
- 2 teaspoons garam masala
- 1/4 cup garlic, minced
- 1 teaspoon dried turmeric
- 1/2 teaspoon cayenne pepper
- 6 russets, peeled and chopped into 1" pieces
- 2 medium head cauliflower, cut into florets
- 2 cups low-sodium vegetable broth
- kosher salt
- freshly ground black pepper
- freshly chopped cilantro, for serving

DIRECTIONS

1. In a huge skillet over medium-high heat, heat oil. Add chili, garlic, and ginger and prepare until fragrant, 1 minute. Add garam masala, turmeric, and cayenne and prepare until toasted, 1 minute even more. Add potatoes, cauliflower, and vegetable broth and time of year with salt and pepper. Reduce heat and make, protected, until potatoes and cauliflower are tender, quarter-hour. Garnish with cilantro to provide.

CARLA LALLI MUSIC

Servings: 10
INGREDIENTS

- 2 1/2-inch piece fresh ginger, unpeeled, coarsely grated
- 1/4 cup loose strong black tea or 6 tea bags (such as tips)
- 28 green cardamom pods, lightly crushed, or 3/4 teaspoon cardamom seeds, lightly crushed
- 2 3-inch cinnamon sticks, lightly crushed with the flat side of a knife
- 5 1/2 cups milk
- 1/2 cup pure maple syrup

DIRECTIONS

1. Bring ginger, cinnamon, and 3½ cups normal water to a boil in an average saucepan on a lot more than medium-high high temperature. Decrease warmth and simmer quickly, stirring occasionally, until liquid is reduced by a third and intensely fragrant, about 20 minutes.
2. Remove pan from warmth, mix in tea and cardamom, and permit steep 2 minutes.
3. Keep coming back pan to medium-high warmth and combine in milk and maple syrup. Cook, stirring occasionally and keeping a close watch until mixture begins to foam up and boil about 5 minutes. Immediately remove from warmth and allow sit for 5 minutes. Tension chai through a fine-mesh sieve into a teapot or pitcher and offer.

BABY BACK RIBS WITH TAMARIND GLAZE

Servings: 10

INGREDIENTS

- 4 racks pork ribs baby back pork ribs (3½–4 pounds total) halved crosswise
- 2 oranges orange wedge (about ⅛ of orange)
- 10 star anise pods
- 2/3 pound ginger ginger peeled chopped
- 4 cups apple juice unfiltered apple juice
- 2 tablespoons salt Diamond Crystal or 2 teaspoons Morton kosher salt
- 12 habanero chiles halved lengthwise seeds removed if desired divided
- cup light brown sugar ¼ plus ⅓ (lightly packed) light brown sugar
- cup ketchup ½ ketchup
- cup cider vinegar ⅓ apple cider vinegar
- cup ¼ tamarind concentrate
- 6 tablespoons honey honey
- vegetable oil Vegetable oil (for grill)
- salt Kosher salt
- 2 cucumbers Persian cucumber thinly sliced

- red onion ½ small red onion thinly sliced
- serrano chile ½ serrano chile very thinly sliced
- 1 1/2 tablespoons lime juice fresh lime juice
- sprig cilantro Micro cilantro and/or cilantro and lime wedges (for serving)
- can Often labeled "concentrate cooking tamarind" or "paste" tamarind concentrate be found at Asian markets and online.

DIRECTIONS

1. Place ribs in a sizable Dutch oven or various other large pots. Add ginger, orange wedge, superstar anise, apple juice, salt, fifty percent of chiles, and ¼ glass dark brown sugar. Pour in drinking water merely to cover pork and provide to a simmer over moderate heat. Reduce heat therefore liquid is at an extremely mild simmer, partially cover the pot, and braise, turning racks several times until meats are fork-tender and almost (however, not quite) dropping off the bones, 1½-2 hours. Chop staying chiles while ribs are cooking food and set aside.

2. Cautiously transfer ribs to a rimmed baking sheet and let cool. Cut between ribs to produce 2-rib pieces.

3. Meanwhile, crank up the heat beneath the Dutch oven to high and put ketchup, vinegar, tamarind focus, honey, remaining ⅓ cup dark brown sugar, and reserved chopped chiles to braising liquid. Cook, stirring frequently until glaze is solid enough to coat a spoon (it must be reduced to 1-1½ cups), 30-45 minutes. Stress into a huge measuring glass; discard solids. Allow settle so essential oil rises to the surface area. Pour off essential oil into a little bowl; set aside.

4. Do Ahead: Ribs could be braised one day ahead. Let awesome in liquid; cover and chill.

5. Make a grill for moderate heat; oil grate. Functioning individually, dip ribs into the glaze to coating. Grill ribs, turning many times, until glaze is usually lightly charred, about five minutes total. Transfer ribs to a platter; time of year with salt. Drizzle with staying glaze and reserved essential oil.

6. Toss cucumber, onion, chile, and lime juice in a moderate bowl to combine; time of year with salt. Scatter salad over ribs and best with micro cilantro. Serve with lime wedges.

CHEDDAR CHEESE-STUFFED KULCHA

Servings: 10

INGREDIENTS

- 1 teaspoon dry active yeast
- 8 cups plus 3 tbsp. (1 1/4 lb.) all-purpose flour, plus more for dusting
- 1 1/2 tablespoons . fine sea salt, divided
- 2 tbsp. plus 1/2 tsp. sugar, divided
- 2 tbsp. canola oils, plus more for greasing
- 8 cups (1 lb.) grated cheddar
- 2 large red bell pepper, finely diced (1 cup)

- 2 tbsp. ground cumin
- 1 teaspoon cayenne pepper
- melted ghee, for brushing
- tomato tadka or chutney, for serving (optional)

DIRECTIONS

1. In the bowl of a stand mixer installed with a dough hook, combine the yeast with 1/2 teaspoon sugar and 1 tablespoon plus 1 1/2 teaspoons lukewarm water. Reserve prior to the yeast provides helped type little bubbles at the top of the water, about five minutes.

2. Add 1 1/4 cups of cold water to the yeast mixture, accompanied simply by the flour, keeping sugar, and 2 1/4 teaspoons salt. Blend on the cheapest velocity until a dough begins to create, 3-3 1/2 occasions. At the moment, if all the flour isn't hydrated and the dough appears extremely dry, add 1-2 extra tablespoons of cold water and mix on low velocity for 30 seconds a lot more. Increase to the next velocity and combine before dough is simple and elastic, 2 occasions more. Decrease the velocity once more, add the canola gas, and mix prior to the oil is equally integrated and the dough is normally homogenous, 2-3 occasions. (The dough should be very sticky and simple, but very smooth.)

3. Lightly oil a medium bowl with canola oil. Transfer the dough to the bowl, turning it over many times to thoroughly covering with the essential oil. Cover the bowl firmly with plastic material and reserve at space temperature before dough is usually inflated, extremely gassy, and nearly doubled in proportions, 80-90 minutes.

4. Generously dust a clean countertop with flour and switch the dough away from any of it. Divide the dough into 5 comparatives (6-oz.) items, softly rounding each into a ball.

5. Lightly oil an enormous baking sheet with canola oil place the dough rounds at the very top, spacing them similarly. Cover tightly with plastic-type material wrap and refrigerate for at least 8 hours or even more to 2 days.

6. One hour before you'll be prepared to bake, preheat a pizza organic stone in a 500° oven. In a moderate bowl, combine the cheese, bell pepper, cumin, cayenne, and remaining 1/4 teaspoon salt; reserve.

7. When the rock is heated, generously flour a countertop. Get rid of the dough from the refrigerator and place among the balls of dough on the floured surface (cover all of those other balls with a clean towel or sheet of the plastic-type material wrap in order to avoid them from blow drying when you work). Make usage of a rolling pin to flatten one little dough out to a 10-in. circle. Pile 1 cup of cheese completing a concise mound at the guts of the circle, from then on pleat the sides up to meet at the guts to seal the cheese within the pouch of dough. Continue filling all those additional balls. Allow stand at least 30 mins before rolling out the kulcha. (Alternately, you can cover and refrigerate the stuffed balls overnight.)

8. Working separately, lightly flour the kulcha, flatten gently, then roll again away to even 8-inches rounds. (If any atmosphere bubbles are trapped within, slit the dough with the finish of a sharpened knife, deflate the bubble, and pinch the beginning back again jointly to seal.) Repeat with all of that

other kulcha.

9. Working quickly to make sure that the oven won't lose temperature among loading, utilize the hands or a pizza peel to transfer 2-3 3 kulchas to your pizza rock. (Bake as many pieces as a possible match on the rock without overlapping or crowding.) Immediately close the oven and bake 5-7 mins, until it truly is irregularly puffed and browned in areas underneath and the cheese within is obviously thoroughly melted.

10. Make usage of a spatula or pizza peel to remove the kulcha and transfer it to a clean baking sheet. Brush softly with ghee and cover with a dry out towel when you keep up baking all that other kulcha.

11. Serve warm, fundamental, or with tomato tadka or chutney privately.

ANDY BARAGHANI

Servings: 10

INGREDIENTS

- 16 scallions (about 1 bunch), divided
- 6 garlic cloves, smashed
- 2 3-inch piece ginger, peeled, smashed to pieces, thinly sliced
- 8 skinless, boneless chicken breasts (about 2 1/4 pounds)
- 1/4 cup mild curry powder
- 2 tablespoons diamond crystal or 1 3/4 teaspoons morton kosher salt, divided, plus more
- juice from 1 orange (about 1/4 cup)
- juice from 1 lime (about 2 tablespoons)
- freshly ground black pepper
- warm jasmine rice (for serving)

DIRECTIONS

1. Coarsely chop 4 scallions and transfer to a medium pot. Add chicken, garlic, ginger, curry powder, 2½ tsp. salt, and 4 cups water. Gradually provide to a bare simmer over moderate heat. Once the liquid starts to simmer, reduce the warmth to low and make until juices run obviously when the thickest component of chicken is definitely pierced, 10-12 minutes.

2. Meanwhile, thinly slice the remaining scallions. Whisk orange juice and lime juice in a little bowl; time of year with salt and 8 turns of a pepper mill, or around ¾ tsp. (you will want a large amount of pepper!).

3. Transfer chicken to a cutting plank and let great slightly. Stress poaching liquid through a fine-mesh sieve into a little bowl. Cut chicken crosswise into slim slices.

4. Divide rice and chicken among bowls and best with sliced scallions. Spoon poaching liquid plus some of the citrus juice over chicken and rice before serving.

5. Do Ahead: Chicken could be poached 2 days forward. Allow chicken and curry great individually. Wrap

chicken and transfer curry to an airtight container; chill.

ASHA GOMEZ

Servings: 10

INGREDIENTS

- 6 tablespoons vegetable oil, divided
- 3 pounds beef chuck, cut into 1' pieces
- kosher salt
- 2 teaspoons coarsely ground black pepper plus more for seasonings
- 10 garlic cloves, chopped
- 2 1x1-inch piece ginger, peeled, thinly sliced
- 2 teaspoons ground turmeric
- 6 serrano chiles, seeded, chopped
- 6 cups low-salt chicken broth
- 1 pound small carrots, scrubbed or peeled, halved lengthwise
- 1 pound baby red-skinned potatoes (about 1 1/2'-diameter), halved, or quartered if large
- 1/2 pound frozen, thawed pearl onions, halved
- 4 cups canned unsweetened coconut milk
- sprig cilantro

DIRECTIONS

1. Heat 1 1/2 Tbsp. the essential oil in a big large pot over medium-high temperature. Period beef with salt and pepper. Employed in 2 batches and adding staying 1 1/2 Tbsp. essential oil between batches, add beef and sear, turning sometimes until browned on all sides, about five minutes. Transfer beef to a plate.
2. Mix in garlic, chiles, and ginger and make, stirring often, until fragrant, about 2 minutes. Add 1 tsp. pepper and turmeric; cook, stirring continuously, until fragrant, about 1 minute. Add broth and reserved beef; provide to a boil, scraping up any browned bits from underneath of pot. Reduce temperature to medium-low, cover pot, and simmer, stirring sometimes, until beef is certainly tender, about 45 minutes.
3. Insert carrots, potatoes, and onions. Cover and simmer, stirring sometimes, until vegetables are tender, 15-20 minutes. Mix in coconut milk.
4. Divide among bowls. Garnish with cilantro.

CHICKEN BIRYANI (30 MINUTE INDIAN CHICKEN & RICE)

Servings: 8

INGREDIENTS

- 2 pounds chicken, cut into strips
- 1/4 cup flour
- 1 teaspoon pepper
- 1 1/2 tablespoons yellow curry powder
- 2 teaspoons kosher salt
- 1/4 cup 2-3 olive oil
- 2 large onions, chopped
- 10 large carrots, sliced
- 1/4 cup 2-3 garlic, smashed and minced
- 1/4 cup yellow curry powder
- 2 teaspoons ginger powder
- 4 cups dry basmati rice
- 6 and 1/2 cups water
- 1 1/2 tablespoons kosher salt
- 1/4 cup butter
- 1 cup cilantro, chopped
- 1 cup cashews, chopped

DIRECTIONS

1. Start by slicing the poultry into strips. Pat the poultry dry out with paper towels. In just a little bowl, combine flour, 1 teaspoon salt, pepper, and 2 teaspoons yellowish curry powder. Dredge each little poultry in the flour mixture to level. In a big, high sided skillet, temperature 1 tablespoon coconut oil over moderate-high temperatures until it shimmers. Add the poultry to the pan one strip simultaneously, with about 1 inch among each little chicken, to supply it a great sear. Do this in at least 2 batches. If you group your poultry into the pan at the same time, it will steam instead of sear, and you may not really get those tasty darkish marks. Cook the poultry on the first factor for about 1-3 a couple of minutes, until browned, from then on the flip with tongs and sear however for 1-2 a couple of minutes until browned. It's alright if the chicken is still raw in the guts, in fact, that's preferable. It'll complete food preparation with the rice. Get rid of the poultry to a plate and reserve. Swirl another tablespoon of coconut oil into the scorching pan. Add the lower onions and saute for 3-5 a couple of minutes. Meanwhile, chop the carrots (discover photos) and place them in a moderate bowl with 1 tablespoon of normal water. Microwave on high for about 3-5 a couple of minutes. The carrots should be softening at this time but nevertheless inflexible. Add the carrots (and liquid) to the pan with the onions. Continue cooking 1-2 a couple of minutes. Add the garlic and saute for 1 minute, until fragrant. Add 2 tablespoons of curry powder and 1 teaspoon ginger, and mix everything together to make sure that the spices get amazing and toasty. Continue food preparation for another 1-2 a couple of minutes. Mix in the rice. Add the normal

water and 2 teaspoons of salt. Mix it jointly and add the poultry back again to the pan. Cover firmly with a lid and convert temperature up to high. Monitor it. When it starts to boil, turn the heat down to low. Produce on low for about 17 a couple of minutes. At this time, the rice must not be crunchy, the carrots tender, and the poultry prepared totally. Place the lid again and keep food preparation for another brief while if it's not necessarily performed. Add 2 tablespoons of butter and mix everything jointly. Stir in lower cilantro and lower cashews. You might mix in golden raisins if you wanted, that could be delicious! Serve with plain yogurt and cucumbers. You may serve it with Roti (Buttery Indian Flatbread) or Homemade Naan.

GAJAR KA HALWA (PUNJABI-STYLE CARROT PUDDING)

Servings: 8

INGREDIENTS

- 2 cups ghee
- 8 carrots medium carrots coarsely grated
- 2 cups sugar
- 2 cups heavy cream heavy cream
- 6 cups milk whole milk
- 2 teaspoons cardamom 1/2 ground green cardamom
- 2 teaspoons water rose water
- 1/4 cup golden raisins golden raisins
- 1/4 cup roughly chopped cashews
- 2 tablespoons almonds roughly chopped almonds
- 2 teaspoons minced pistachios

DIRECTIONS

1. Melt 1/3 glass ghee in a 12" nonstick skillet over medium-high heat; mix in carrots. Add milk; boil. Reduce high temperature to medium; make, stirring sometimes, until carrots are extremely tender and sauce is normally thickened, 30-35 minutes. Mix in sugar, cream, cardamom, and rose drinking water; prepare until sugar is normally dissolved and halwa is normally heavy about 25 minutes.

2. Melt remaining ghee within an 8" skillet over medium-high high temperature; prepare raisins, cashews, and almonds until raisins are plump and nuts are lightly toasted, 3-4 minutes. Stir mix into halwa and garnish with pistachios; serve at area temperature.

CHICKEN CURRY

Servings: 10

INGREDIENTS

- 1/4 cup extra-virgin olive oil
- 2 medium yellow onions, chopped
- 6 tablespoons garlic, minced
- 2 tablespoons minced ginger
- 4 pounds . boneless skinless chicken breasts, cut into 1" pieces
- 1 tablespoon . paprika
- 1 tablespoon . ground turmeric
- 1 tablespoon . ground coriander
- 2 teaspoons ground cumin
- 2 cans 1 (15-oz.) crushed tomatoes
- 3 cups . low-sodium chicken broth
- 1 cup heavy cream
- kosher salt
- freshly ground black pepper
- basmati rice or naan, for serving
- 2 tablespoons freshly chopped cilantro, for garnish

DIRECTIONS

1. In a big pot over medium-high heat, heat oil. Add onion and make until smooth, 5 minutes. Add poultry and sear until no pink is still, five minutes. Mix in garlic and ginger and prepare until fragrant, 1 minute. Add spices and prepare until incredibly fragrant, 1 minute. Add tomatoes and broth and offer to a simmer. Mix in large cream and period with salt and pepper. Simmer until poultry parts are ready through and tender, about 15 to 20 a couple of minutes. Serve over rice or with naan, garnished with cilantro.

BEEF CURRY

Servings: 10

INGREDIENTS

- 4 pounds . beef chuck, cut into 1 1/2-inch pieces
- kosher salt
- freshly ground black pepper
- 2 medium onions, diced
- 8 garlic cloves, finely grated
- 4 tablespoons vegetable oil

- 6 pieces " ginger, finely grated
- 1 teaspoon ground cinnamon
- 1/2 teaspoon cayenne
- 6 tablespoons curry powder
- 4 cans 2 (13.5-oz) unsweetened coconut milk
- yogurt, for serving
- naan, for serving
- lime wedges, for serving

DIRECTIONS

1. Season meats generously with salt and pepper. In a sizable skillet over moderate-high heat, heat essential oil. Add beef and prepare, flipping once, until deeply golden, three to five 5 minutes per aspect. Transfer to a plate. Add onion to skillet and make until soft, about five minutes. Add garlic, ginger, and spices and prepare until fragrant, 1 minute. Add coconut milk and provide to a simmer. Decrease high temperature to low, add beef, and continue steadily to simmer until fork-tender, about 1 1/2 hours. Serve with yogurt, naan, and lime wedges.

ASHA GOMEZ, CHEF AT CARDAMOM HILL IN ATLANTA

Servings: 10

INGREDIENTS

- 4 serrano chiles, stemmed
- 4 garlic cloves, finely chopped
- 1 cup fresh cilantro leaves with tender stems
- 2/3 cup fresh mint leaves
- 4 cups buttermilk
- 1/4 cup finely chopped peeled ginger
- 1/4 cup kosher salt
- 24 skin-on, bone-in chicken pieces (about 6 lb.)
- vegetable oil (for frying)
- 4 cups all-purpose flour
- 1/4 cup virgin coconut oils
- 8 stems fresh curry leaves, leaves separated
- fresh peach chutney (click for recipe; for serving)
- a deep-fry thermometer

DIRECTIONS

1. Purée chiles, garlic, buttermilk, cilantro, mint, ginger, and salt in a blender until clean. Place poultry in a huge bowl, add buttermilk blend and toss to mix. Cover and chill at least 4 hours and ideally 24 hours.
2. Fit a huge cast-iron skillet or additional heavy straight-sided skillet (not nonstick) with deep-fry thermometer; pour in vegetable essential oil to measure 1" and heat over medium-high temperature until thermometer registers 325°.
3. Place flour in a shallow bowl. Remove poultry from marinade, scraping off excess, and pat dried out. Dredge poultry in flour, shaking off excess. Employed in 2 batches, fry poultry, turning frequently with tongs and adjusting the temperature to keep up temperature between 325°-350°, until pores and skin is definitely deep golden brownish and an instant-examine thermometer inserted into the thickest component of chicken registers 165°, 10-12 mins for wings and 12-15 mins for thighs, hip and legs, and breasts. Transfer poultry to a cable rack set in the baking sheet and brush with coconut essential oil.
4. Fry curry leaves in veggie oil until sizzling, about 1 minute; transfer to a paper towel-lined plate.
5. Serve poultry with fried curry leaves and peach chutney.

CHICKEN TIKKA MASALA

Servings: 10

INGREDIENTS

- 2 tablespoons extra-virgin olive oil
- 2 pounds . boneless skinless chicken breasts, cut into 1" cubes
- 2/3 cup garlic, minced
- 2 tablespoons freshly minced ginger
- 2 onions, chopped
- 1 teaspoon ground turmeric
- 1 1/2 tablespoons ground cumin
- 1 1/2 tablespoons paprika
- 1 1/2 tablespoons garam masala
- 2 teaspoons cayenne pepper
- 2 cans 1 (28-oz.) crushed tomatoes
- 1 cup plus 2 tbs heavy cream
- kosher salt
- freshly chopped cilantro, for garnish
- rice or naan, for serving

DIRECTIONS

1. In a huge skillet over moderate heat, heat oil. Add chicken and make, flipping once, until golden no longer pink, 8 minutes per part. Transfer to a plate. Add onion to skillet and make until soft, about five minutes. Add garlic, ginger, and spices and prepare until fragrant, 1 minute. Add tomatoes and simmer

until thickened, about a quarter-hour. Add large cream and poultry and simmer until warmed through, five minutes more. Period with salt. Garnish with cilantro and provide alongside rice or naan, if using.

GOAN FISH CURRY

Servings: 10

INGREDIENTS

- 4 pounds . boneless, skinless cod fillet, cut into 1-inch pieces
- 6 tablespoons fresh lemon juice
- kosher salt
- 2 large yellow onions, finely chopped
- 6 tablespoons garlic, mashed into a paste
- 6 tablespoons vegetable oil
- 2 (2-inch) piece ginger, mashed into a paste
- 1 tablespoon . ground coriander
- 2 teaspoons ground cumin
- 1 teaspoon chile powder
- 1 teaspoon ground turmeric
- 6 tablespoons white wine vinegar
- 4 small green chiles, thinly sliced
- 2 (13.5-ounce) can coconut milk
- fresh cilantro, to garnish
- cooked basmati or long grain rice, for serving

DIRECTIONS

1. Toss seafood with lemon juice and salt in a moderate bowl; cover with plastic material wrap and refrigerate for 20 minutes.
2. Temperature oil in a 12-inch skillet more than medium-high; add onion and make, stirring occasionally, until smooth, about 6 mins. Add garlic and ginger pastes and prepare 1 minute much longer. Add coriander, cumin, chile powder, and turmeric and prepare 1 minute even more. Add vinegar, sliced chiles, and the coconut milk and simmer, stirring sometimes, 6-8 minutes.
3. Add the fish and simmer lightly until the fish is prepared, 4-5 mins. Remove from temperature and divide among plates; best with cilantro and serve with rice.

CHICKEN VINDALOO

Servings: 8

INGREDIENTS

- 2 tbsp. whole black peppercorns
- 2 tbsp. black mustard seeds
- 1 1/2 tablespoons coriander seeds
- 2 teaspoons fenugreek seeds
- 1 1/2 tablespoons cumin seeds
- 10 whole cloves
- 1 cup 1 (1") cinnamon
- 1/2 cup hungarian paprika
- 1/2 cup palm vinegar
- 2 teaspoons ground turmeric
- 2 teaspoons light brown sugar
- 2 cups garlic, minced
- 2 pieces 1 (2") ginger, peeled and minced
- 4 pounds . boneless, skinless chicken thighs, cut in half
- 6 tbsp. canola oil
- 4 large yellow onions, finely chopped
- 20 thin green indian chiles, stemmed, seeded, and minced
- 2 pounds . small new potatoes, cut in half (cut in quarters if large)
- cooked white rice, for serving

DIRECTIONS

1. Temperature peppercorns, mustard, cumin, coriander, and fenugreek seeds, cloves, and cinnamon in a 12" skillet over medium-high temperature, and cook, swirling pan occasionally, until lightly toasted, about 2 mins. Transfer to a bowl, and let cool; employed in batches, transfer spices to a spice grinder and procedure until finely surface. Transfer to a little food processor chip along with paprika, vinegar, turmeric, sugar, 1/4 of the garlic, and fifty percent the ginger; puree until simple. Transfer to a sizable bowl, and add poultry; rub poultry with the spice blend. Cover and refrigerate at least 4 hours or up to overnight.

2. Temperature oil in a 6-qt. saucepan over medium-high temperature. Add onions, and prepare, stirring, until caramelized, about 25 mins. Add staying garlic and ginger along with chiles, and prepare, stirring, until soft, about five minutes. Add poultry along with any paste in a bowl, potatoes, and 2 cups drinking water, and provide to a boil; decrease the temperature to medium-low, and make, covered and stirring sometimes until poultry is cooked through about 25 mins. Remove from temperature, and period with salt; serve with rice.

GREEN CHUTNEY WITH CHAAT MASALA

Servings: 10

INGREDIENTS

- 2 1/2-inch piece ginger, peeled, chopped
- 2 jalapeño, seeds removed, chopped
- 3 cups mint leaves
- 2/3 cup plain whole-milk greek yogurt
- 3 cups cilantro leaves with tender stems
- 2 1/2 tablespoons fresh lemon juice
- 2 1/2 tablespoons vegetable oil
- 2 teaspoons chaat masala
- kosher salt

DIRECTIONS

1. Pulse ginger, jalapeño, cilantro, mint, yogurt, lemon juice, essential oil, and chaat masala in a meals processor until smooth; period with salt.

DIANE FIELDS

Servings: 10

INGREDIENTS

- 7 3/4 cups of garlic
- 2 tablespoons extra-virgin olive oil
- kosher salt, freshly ground pepper
- 2 cups plain low-fat yogurt
- 1/2 cup finely chopped, peeled, seeded cucumbers
- 1/2 teaspoon cumin seeds
- 2 teaspoons chopped fresh cilantro
- 2 teaspoons chopped fresh mint
- 2 teaspoons minced seeded jalapeño
- 1 teaspoon (or more) fresh lemon juice
- 1 cup mixed dried legumes (such as lentils and whole mung beans)
- 1/2 cup basmati rice
- 2 garlic cloves, minced
- 2 teaspoons chopped peeled fresh ginger
- 1 jalapeño, seeded, minced
- 2 cups leaves from pea tendrils, arugula, or spinach, chopped
- 1 cup peas (from about 8 ounces peas in pods), chopped

- 1/2 cup chopped fresh cilantro
- 1/2 cup chopped scallions
- 6 tablespoons chopped fresh mint
- 2 teaspoons kosher salt
- 2 teaspoons freshly ground black pepper
- 1/2 cup extra-virgin olive oils, divided

DIRECTIONS

1. Preheat oven to 450°. Cut top 1/2" off the mind of garlic; discard. Place garlic on a sheet of foil. Drizzle with essential oil; sprinkle with salt and pepper. Wrap in foil. Roast until tender, about 45 minutes. Let awesome. Squeeze cloves from skins, keeping cloves intact.

2. Stir cumin in a little dry skillet over moderate heat until deep dark brown, 2-3 minutes. Let awesome. Finely grind in a spice mill.

3. Blend yogurt, cucumber, cilantro, mint, jalapeño, and 1/2 teaspoon lemon juice in a moderate bowl. Mix in cumin. Time of year with salt, pepper, and even more lemon juice, if preferred.

4. Wash legumes; place in a moderate bowl with rice. Add drinking water to cover by 3". Allow legumes and rice soak at space temperature for 3-5 hours.

5. Drain legumes and rice; transfer to a meals processor chip. Add garlic, ginger, and jalapeño. Procedure until grainy paste forms (add 1-2 tablespoons water if required). Transfer to a huge bowl; blend in tendrils and then 6 **INGREDIENTS**.

6. Heat 1 tablespoon essential oil in a huge nonstick skillet over medium-high warmth. Spoon 4 scant 1/4-cupfuls of batter into skillet, flattening with the trunk of a measuring glass into 1/4"-solid cakes. Reduce warmth to moderate; sauté until golden brownish and prepared through, adding 1 more tablespoon essential oil when cakes are flipped, about 4-5 moments per side. Do it again with the remaining essential oil and batter. Divide raita among plates; best with roasted garlic cloves. Place 2 cakes on each plate.

GOAN COCONUT CAKE (BAATH)

Servings: 4

INGREDIENTS

- 2 cups semolina
- 1/2 teaspoon baking powder
- 1/8 teaspoon fine sea salt
- 1 1/4 cups superfine sugar
- 2 eggs
- 2 tablespoons coconut oils
- 4 tbsp. unsalted butter, softened, plus more for greasing

- 33 cans 1 (13 1/2-oz.) coconut milk
- 2 tablespoons cream of coconut
- 3/4 teaspoon . rosewater
- 1/2 cup unsweetened shredded coconut

DIRECTIONS

1. Collection an 8-by-8-inch square cake pan with parchment paper; grease with butter, then reserve.
2. Whisk flour, baking powder, and salt in a bowl; in a huge bowl, defeat sugar, coconut essential oil, and butter on the moderate speed of a hands mixer until fluffy, about three minutes. Add eggs individually, beating after every addition until easy. Add fifty percent of the coconut milk and cream of coconut, after that half the dry elements, and beat until simply combined; add in staying coconut milk and cream of coconut, in addition to the rosewater, blending well to mix. Add remaining dry substances and combine well; fold in shredded coconut, after that pour batter equally into ready pan. Cover with plastic material wrap, then refrigerate overnight.
3. The very next day, heat the oven to 350°. Unwrap cake, after that bake, turning halfway through, until golden brown, about 90 minutes. Great cake completely before slicing and serving.

HOMEMADE NAAN

Servings: 10

INGREDIENTS

- 2 cups warm water (about 110°f)
- 1/4 cup honey
- 7 cups all-purpose flour
- 1/2 cup plain yogurt
- 2 (0.25 ounce) package active dry yeast (about 2 1/4 teaspoons)
- 1 1/2 tablespoons fine sea salt
- 1 teaspoon baking powder
- 2 large eggs
- 1/2 cup salted butter
- 6 tablespoons garlic, peeled and minced
- finely- chopped fresh cilantro or parsley
- (optional) flaky sea salt

DIRECTIONS

1. Activate the yeast: Briefly mix together the hot water and honey in the plate of a stand mixer. (Or see notes below about how exactly to help make the dough yourself.) Sprinkle the yeast along with the water and present it an instant stir, then allow mixture rest for 5-10 minutes before yeast is foamy.
2. Combine the dough: Add the flour, yogurt, salt, baking powder, and egg. Using the dough attachment,

combine the dough on medium-low speed for 2-3 minutes until even. (The dough it's still slightly sticky, but should form right into a ball that pulls from the sides of the blending bowl. If it's as well sticky, add a little more flour.)

3. Allow dough rise. Remove dough from the blending bowl and use the hands to type it right into a ball. Grease the blending bowl (or another bowl) lightly with cooking food spray, after that place the dough ball back in the bowl and cover it with a damp towel. Place the bowl in a warm area (I established mine by a sunny screen) and allow it to rise for one hour before the dough has almost doubled in size.

4. (Optional) Make the garlic butter: Over the last ten minutes of the dough's rise period, the high temperature the butter in a little sauté pan over moderate-high temperature until melted. Add the garlic and make for 1-2 a few minutes until fragrant. Take away the pain from high temperature and stir in a few chopped herbal remedies, if desired. (You can even stress out the garlic chunks if you like the garlic butter to end up being completely smooth.)

5. Roll out the dough. After the dough is preparing to move, transfer it to a floured work surface area and form it into a straight(ish) circle. Slice the dough into 8 equally-sized wedges and roll each wedge right into a ball together with your hands. After that make use of a rolling pin to roll out the dough ball until it forms an oval about 1/4-inch heavy. (I would recommend multi-tasking this technique - rolling out another dough ball when you make one on the stove.)

6. Cook the dough. High temperature a sizable cast-iron skillet or non-stay sauté pan over medium-high heat. Put in a little bit of the rolled-out dough to the pan and make for 1 minute, or before the surface of the dough starts to bubble and underneath turns lightly golden. Flip the dough and prepare on the next side for 30-60 seconds, or before the bottom is golden as well, after that transfer the dough to a clean plate. (In case you are producing garlic naan, brush one or both aspect(s) of the dough with the garlic butter after the naan has prepared.) Sprinkle the naan with a pinch of flaky ocean salt, if desired. After that gently cover the naan with a towel to ensure that it stays warm. Do it again with staying dough until all the naan parts are cooked.

7. Serve. Serve warm and revel in!

GREEN PAPAYA

Servings: 8

INGREDIENTS

- 6 tbsp. fresh or frozen grated coconut
- 1/4 cup garlic, peeled
- 2 small green thai chile or 1/2 serrano, stemmed
- 2 teaspoons cumin seeds
- 2 medium red onions, minced
- kosher salt, to taste

- 1/2 cup coconut or canola oil
- 2 teaspoons black mustard seeds
- 1 1/2 tablespoons ground turmeric
- 2 small green papayas, peeled, seeded, and minced
- 1 teaspoon red chile powder, such as cayenne
- 20 curry leaves

DIRECTIONS

1. Purée coconut, cumin seeds, garlic, chile, fifty percent the onion, and salt in a little food processor right into a paste.

2. Temperature oil in a 12" skillet over medium-high. Make mustard seeds until they pop, 1-2 mins. Cook staying onion until golden, 4-6 minutes. Mix in the turmeric, papaya, and salt; make, protected, until papaya is merely tender, about a quarter-hour. Mix in reserved coconut paste, the chile powder, and curry leaves; make, covered and stirring sometimes, until papaya is quite tender and the blend is slightly dry, 18-20 minutes more.

INDIAN FISH AND POTATO CROQUETTES

Servings: 12

INGREDIENTS

- 6 whole cloves
- 4 green cardamom pods
- 2 cinnamon sticks
- 1 pound skinless cod or red snapper fillets
- 2 bay leaves
- 2 pounds . russet potatoes, peeled and cut into 1-inch chunks
- kosher salt
- 1 cup whole-wheat bread crumbs
- 4 tbsp. fresh lime juice
- 4 tbsp. roughly chopped cilantro
- 2 teaspoons ground cumin
- 2 small green indian chile or serrano, stemmed, seeded, and minced (optional)
- 1/2 cup vegetable oil
- mint chutney, for serving

DIRECTIONS

1. In a little saucepan, combine the cloves with the cardamom, bay leaf, cinnamon, and 2 cups water and provide to a boil. Add the seafood, go back to a boil, after that reduce the heat to keep up a simmer, and

poach the seafood until cooked through about five minutes. Utilizing a slotted spoon or tongs, transfer the seafood to a bowl, and allow awesomely. Discard the spices and cooking food liquid.

2. Meanwhile, cover the potatoes with generously salted drinking water in a moderate saucepan, provide to a boil, and make until tender, about 20 moments. Drain the potatoes and allow them to cool completely.

3. Add the potatoes to the bowl with the fish combined with the bread crumbs, lime juice, cilantro, cumin, and chile, time of year with salt, and gently mash the potatoes with the additional ingredients until equally combined. Form the mix into six 3-inch-wide, 3/4-inch-thick patties.

4. In a 12-inch nonstick skillet, warm the oil over moderate heat. Add the patties and make, flipping once, until golden dark brown, about 6 a few minutes. Transfer the seafood patties to a serving platter and serve while scorching with mint chutney privately.

GRILLED MUSTARD BROCCOLI

Servings: 10

INGREDIENTS

- 4 small heads of broccoli (about 1 1/2 pounds)
- kosher salt
- 2 tablespoons mustard oil or olive oil
- 2 tablespoons whole grain mustard
- 1 cup plain whole-milk greek yogurt
- 1 tablespoon kashmiri chili powder or paprika
- 2 teaspoons chaat masala
- 2 teaspoons ground cumin
- 2 teaspoons ground turmeric
- vegetable oil (for grill)

DIRECTIONS

1. Trim broccoli stems, after that cut from heads. Peel stems and slices lengthwise into ¼"-solid planks. Split up heads into large florets. Make florets and stems in a huge pot of boiling salted drinking water until shiny green and crisp-tender, about 2 minutes. Drain, after that transfer to a plate of ice water to awesome. Drain and pat dried out with paper towels.

2. Whisk yogurt, mustard essential oil, mustard, chili powder, chaat masala, cumin, and turmeric in a huge bowl. Add broccoli and toss to coat; time of year with salt.

3. Make a grill for medium-high heating; essential oil grate. Grill broccoli, turning sometimes until charred in places, 5-7 moments. Transfer to a platter.

CILANTRO YOGURT CHUTNEY

Servings: 10

INGREDIENTS

- 2 cups plain yogurt
- 2 tbsp. fresh lime juice
- 4 small green thai chilies or 1 serrano, stemmed
- 1 1/2 cups roughly chopped cilantro
- kosher salt, to taste

DIRECTIONS

Purée 1/4 glass yogurt with remaining substances in a little food processor until steady; transfer to a bowl and mix in remaining yogurt.

GULAB JAMUN (CARDAMOM SYRUP-SOAKED DONUTS)

Servings: 8

INGREDIENTS

- 4 cups whole milk
- 1 1/4 cups sugar
- 1/2 teaspoon rosewater
- 4 pods cardamom, cracked
- 1/16 teaspoon saffron
- 2 tablespoons (1 1/4 oz.) all-purpose flour, sifted
- 2 tablespoons semolina flour
- 1/4 teaspoon baking powder
- 1 1/2 tbsp. ghee or clarified butter, plus more for frying
- 1/2 tbsp. plain yogurt
- 1/2 egg

DIRECTIONS

1. Bring milk to a boil in a 4-qt. nonstick pan. Reduce warmth to medium-low; make, stirring, until very solid, about 5 hours. You ought to have 1 1/2 cups of thickened milk; let awesome to room temperature.
2. Bring sugars, saffron, rosewater, cardamom, and 13/4 cups drinking water to a boil in a 1-qt. saucepan. Make, stirring, until sugar dissolves, 8-10 moments; let cool.
3. Combine thickened milk, the flours, and baking powder in a plate of a stand mixer fitted with a paddle attachment; blend. Add ghee, yogurt, and egg; continue steadily to defeat until dough forms. Cover with plastic material wrap and reserve for 10 minutes.
4. High temperature 2" ghee in a 6-qt. pan until a deep-fry thermometer reads 275°. Using wet hands,

divide the dough into 16 parts; roll into balls. Employed in batches, fry, stirring to maintain donuts submerged until prepared through, 12-15 minutes. Utilizing a slotted spoon, transfer to paper towels to drain briefly; transfer scorching donuts to the syrup and allow soak for at least thirty minutes before serving.

GYMKHANA, LONDON

Servings: 10

INGREDIENTS

- 2 pounds new potatoes or small yukon gold potatoes, scrubbed
- kosher salt
- 1 small onion, chopped
- 2 1-inch piece ginger, peeled, chopped
- 1 cup chopped fresh cilantro, plus more for serving
- 2 serrano chile, seeds removed if desired, chopped
- 1/2 cup vegetable oil
- 2 ounces 15.5- can chickpeas, rinsed, patted dry
- freshly ground black pepper
- 1 1/2 tablespoons chaat masala
- 1/4 cup prepared tamarind chutney, divided
- pinch of sugar
- 1 1/2 cups plain whole-milk greek yogurt
- 1/4 cup melted ghee or clarified butter
- 1/2 cup sev (optional)

DIRECTIONS

1. Place potatoes in a huge pot and add drinking water to cover. Bring to a boil, season drinking water with salt, and prepare until fork-tender, 12-15 mins. Drain; set potatoes apart.
2. In the meantime, pulse onion, chile, ginger, and ½ glass cilantro in a meals processor chip to a coarse paste; reserve.
3. Using the palm of your hands, gently crush potatoes (it's okay in the event that the skins split). Temperature oil in a huge skillet over medium-high and add potatoes and chickpeas. Time of year with salt and pepper and toss to coat. Cook, shaking pan sometimes until potatoes and chickpeas are both extremely browned and crisp, 12-15 minutes.
4. Add more masala, reserved cilantro mixture, and 1 Tbsp. tamarind chutney and toss to coating. Make until spices are fragrant and tamarind chutney can be thickened about 2 mins. Transfer to a platter.
5. Mix sugar into yogurt in a little bowl; time of year with salt. Drizzle over potatoes along with ghee and staying 1 Tbsp. tamarind chutney. Best with an increase of cilantro and sev, if using.

HOT MIX (INDIAN SPICED SNACK MIX)

Servings: 10

INGREDIENTS

- 2 cups poha (dried flattened rice flakes)
- 40 fresh or frozen curry leaves, defrosted if frozen
- 2 teaspoons ground turmeric
- 12 chiles de árbol, stemmed and roughly chopped
- 1 cup dried shaved coconut
- 1 cup golden raisins
- 1 cup roasted chana dal (yellow split peas)
- 1 cup sev (fried chickpea noodles)
- 1 cup spicy boondi (fried sweetened chickpea balls)
- 1 cup unsalted pistachios
- 1 cup unsalted roasted cashews
- 1 cup unsalted roasted peanuts
- 1 cup whole almonds
- 3 tbsp. sugar
- 1 tablespoon . red chile powder, such as cayenne
- kosher salt, to taste

DIRECTIONS

1. Temperature oil in a 14" flat-bottom wok more than medium-high. Mix in turmeric and, employed in batches, fry poha until puffed and crisp, 10-15 seconds. Utilizing a slotted spoon, transfer poha to paper towels to drain; transfer to a sizable bowl. Fry curry leaves and chiles until fragrant, about 1 minute; drain in some recoverable format towels and transfer to bowl with the pour. Fry coconut, and raisins, about 30 secs each; drain in some recoverable format towels and transfer to bowl with the pour. Add fried chana dal, noodles, boondi, pistachios, cashews, peanuts, almonds, sugar, reddish colored chile powder, and salt; toss to mix. Store within an air-limited container for up to at least one 1 month.

INDIAN LAMB CURRY IN A BREAD BOWL (BUNNY CHOW)

Servings: 8

INGREDIENTS

- 12 large cloves peeled garlic
- one 3-inch piece peeled fresh ginger

- 4 large white onions, chopped (about 3 cups)
- 8 bay leaves
- 1/2 cup plus 2 tbsp. canola or olive oil
- 4 small cinnamon sticks
- 2 tbsp. ground turmeric
- 1/2 cup plus 1 tbsp. garam masala
- 6 medium tomatoes, chopped (2 cups)
- 4 1/2 pounds . boneless mutton or lamb shoulder, cut into 1-inch cubes
- 4 tbsp. kosher salt
- 6 medium russet potatoes (1 3/4 lb.), peeled and cut into 1-inch cubes
- leaves from 12 sprigs fresh cilantro
- pound one 1- loaf unsliced white bread, cut crosswise into quarters

DIRECTIONS

1. In a little food processor chip or mortar and pestle, add the garlic and ginger and pulse or pound until paste forms. Reserve.

2. In a sizable (8-quart) Dutch oven or heavy-bottomed pot, heat the oil over moderate heat until it shimmers. Add the onions, bay leaves, cinnamon sticks, and turmeric and make, stirring occasionally, before onions are softened about five minutes. Mix in the garam masala and 1/4 glass of the garlic-ginger paste (reserve any staying paste for another make use of); cook for a couple of seconds, stirring to avoid the spices from burning up. Add the tomatoes and provide to a simmer; allow cook for five minutes. Add the mutton and salt, stirring to layer the meats in the sauce, and distribute the seasoning. Simmer, stirring occasionally, a quarter-hour. Mix in the potatoes and 2 cups drinking water; provide to a boil, after that decrease to a simmer. Cook, uncovered before the meat is certainly tender and potatoes are gentle about 40 minutes.

3. To serve, cut away the majority of the center of every bread one fourth and reserve it entirely, making sure to keep some bread at the bottom of every. Divide among 4 plates and fill up the bread bowls with the curry blend. Garnish with the cilantro, and best or provide with the reserved bread parts.

JOANNA CISMARU

Servings: 8

INGREDIENTS

- 2 cups   chickpeas drained
- 2 teaspoons   smoked paprika
- 2 teaspoons garlic powder
- 1/2 teaspoon salt or to taste
- 2 teaspoons cumin

- 1 teaspoon pepper or to taste
- 2   large cauliflower broken into florets
- 2 teaspoons cumin ground
- 2 teaspoons   garam masala *
- 1 teaspoon salt
- 1 teaspoon   ground turmeric **
- 1/2 teaspoon cayenne pepper
- 4 chicken breasts boneless and skinless cut in 1 inch cubes
- 1/4 cup olive oil
- 1/4 cup garlic minced
- 2 teaspoons   fresh ginger grated
- 2   small onions chopped
- 2 cups carrots shredded
- 2 cups peas frozen
- 1/4 cup cilantro for garnish

DIRECTIONS

1. Preheat oven to 400 F degrees. Spray a baking sheet with cooking spray.

2. In a moderate bowl toss jointly the chickpeas with the smoked paprika, cumin, garlic powder, salt, and pepper. Make certain each chickpea is protected in spices. Pass on the chickpeas within an even level over the ready baking sheet.

3. Roast the chickpeas in the oven for approximately 20 to thirty minutes or until dry out and crispy externally.

4. Meanwhile, place the cauliflower florets in a food processor chip and pulse until the blend resembles the consistency of rice. You will likely want to do this in a few batches. Place in a bowl and reserve.

5. In a moderate bowl combine the cumin, garam masala, salt, turmeric, and cayenne pepper. Add the poultry parts and toss and make certain each poultry piece is covered in the spice blend.

6. In a sizable wok or skillet heat 1 tbsp of the essential olive oil over moderate-high heat. Add the minced garlic and ginger and make for 10 secs. Add the poultry to the wok and make for approximately 5 to 6 mins or before the chicken is no pinker and begins to brown a little bit. Stir as necessary to ensure the poultry cooks on all sides.

7. Remove the poultry from the wok. Add the rest of the 1 tbsp of essential olive oil and add onion, carrots, and peas. Make and stir for 2 mins. Add the cauliflower rice and stir well, after that cook for another 4 mins until cauliflower can be tender. Period with salt and pepper if required. Return poultry to work and temperature through.

8. Serve even though warm topped with the roasted chickpeas and cilantro.

INDIAN LENTIL STEW (KHATTI DAL)

Servings: 8

INGREDIENTS

- 2 cups toor dal (yellow pigeon peas), rinsed, soaked 30 minutes, and drained
- 1/2 teaspoon ground turmeric
- 2 teaspoons tamarind paste
- 1/2 teaspoon red chile powder, such as cayenne
- 6 tbsp. chopped cilantro
- 24 fresh or frozen curry leaves
- 1 cup garlic (1 mashed into a paste, 6 peeled)
- 4 plum tomatoes, peeled and minced
- 4 small green thai chiles, or 1 serrano, thinly sliced
- 2 (1/2-inch) piece ginger, peeled and grated
- kosher salt, to taste
- 6 tbsp. canola oil
- 1 teaspoon cumin seeds
- 1/2 teaspoon brown mustard seeds
- 6 chiles de árbol

DIRECTIONS

1. Bring dal and 8 cups drinking water to a boil in a 6-qt. saucepan. Reduce heat to moderate; mix in the turmeric and prepare until dal is definitely mushy about 45 minutes.
2. Mix in cilantro, tamarind paste, chile powder, curry leaves, garlic paste, tomatoes, sliced chiles, ginger, and salt; boil. Reduce warmth to moderate; cook until somewhat thickened, about quarter-hour.
3. Heat oil within an 8" skillet more than medium-high. Make cumin and mustard seeds until they pop, 1-2 moments. Add peeled garlic and the chiles de árbol; cook until garlic is definitely golden, 6-8 moments, and mix into the stew.

KACHI YAKHNI BIRYANI (HYDERABADI-STYLE STEAMED CHICKEN AND RICE)

Servings: 12

INGREDIENTS

- 2 cups canola oil
- 2 large yellow onions, thinly sliced
- 2 cups roughly chopped cilantro

- 2 cups roughly chopped mint
- 2 (3 1/2-4-lb.) chicken, cut into 8 pieces
- 6 tbsp. garam masala
- 2 teaspoons red chile powder, such as cayenne
- 1/2 teaspoon ground turmeric
- 3/4 cup garlic, peeled
- 4 small green thai chiles or 1 serrano, stemmed
- 2 pieces 1 (4") ginger, peeled and thinly sliced
- juice of half a lemon
- kosher salt, to taste
- 4 cups plain, full-fat yogurt
- 1 teaspoon kala jerra (black cumin seeds)
- 6 whole cloves
- 4 green cardamom pods
- 1 cup cinnamon
- 4 cups long-grain white rice
- 1 cup ghee, melted

DIRECTIONS

1. Heat 1 cup essential oil and the onion in a 6-qt. saucepan over medium heat. Make, stirring sometimes, until onion is certainly caramelized, about 25 minutes; utilizing a slotted spoon, transfer onion to a bowl and reserve essential oil for another use.

2. Cut chicken into 18 pieces: Cut poultry into 8 pieces, discarding wingtips. Cut each drumstick, thigh, and wing in two and cut each breast crosswise into 3 parts; transfer to a bowl.

3. Purée 1/3 the reserved onion, the cilantro, mint, garam masala, chile powder, turmeric, garlic, green chiles, ginger, lemon juice, and salt in a little food processor right into a paste; arranged half the paste apart. Add staying paste to the bowl with poultry. Add yogurt; toss to mix. Cover with plastic material wrap; chill one hour.

4. Clean pan clean and put cumin, cloves, cardamom, cinnamon, and 6 cups drinking water; boil. Mix in rice; prepare until rice is somewhat tender, about five minutes. Stress rice and spices, discarding drinking water. Spoon 1/3 the rice and spice combination into pan; best with half the poultry and its own marinade. Sprinkle with fifty percent the rest of the herb paste, drizzle with 1/3 the ghee, and sprinkle 1/3 the rest of the onion over top. Do it again layering the rest of the rice, poultry, herb paste, and ghee. Steam, protected, on low warmth until rice and poultry are completely cooked, 35-40 moments. Garnish with staying caramelized onion.

INDIAN LIME RICE

Servings: 8

INGREDIENTS

- 2 cups basmati rice, rinsed until water runs clear
- 3 tbsp. chana dal (yellow split peas), rinsed until water runs clear
- 1/2 cup canola oil
- 1/2 teaspoon ground turmeric
- 24 fresh or frozen curry leaves
- 2 teaspoons black mustard seeds
- 1/2 cup garlic, thinly sliced
- 8 small green thai chiles or 2 serranos, roughly chopped
- 1/2 teaspoon asafoetida
- 1/2 cup fresh lime juice
- kosher salt, to taste

DIRECTIONS

1. Bring 6 cups of drinking water to a boil in a 4-qt. saucepan. Add rice; make, stirring sometimes, until rice is certainly tender, 10-12 a few minutes. Meanwhile, combine dal and 1 cup drinking water in a bowl; allow sit 30 minutes, after that drain. Drain the rice and transfer to a bowl. Add essential oil to pan; high temperature over medium-high. Make mustard seeds until they pop, 1-2 a few minutes. Add reserved dal; prepare until reddish-brown, 5-7 a few minutes. Add turmeric, curry leaves, garlic, and chiles; prepare until garlic is certainly golden, 2-3 a few minutes. Add asafoetida; stir into rice with lime juice and salt.

MAACHER JHOL (BENGALI-STYLE FISH STEW)

Servings: 8

INGREDIENTS

- 2 pounds . boneless, skin-on catfish, trout, or salmon, cut into 2" pieces
- 1/2 teaspoon ground turmeric
- kosher salt, to taste
- 3 tbsp. black mustard seeds
- 2 tbsp. cumin seeds
- 2/3 cup mustard oils
- 1 1/2 tablespoons panch phoran (bengali five-spice powder)
- 4 small green thai chiles or 1 serrano, halved
- 6 tablespoons garlic, mashed into a paste

- 2 pieces 1 (2") ginger, peeled and mashed into a paste
- 2 small red onions, minced
- 4 plum tomatoes, chopped
- 2/3 cup packed cilantro leaves

DIRECTIONS

1. Rub seafood with turmeric and salt in a bowl. Warmth a 6-qt. saucepan over medium-high; make mustard and cumin seeds until they pop, 1-2 moments. Grind in a spice grinder right into a powder. Add essential oil to pan; warmth over medium-high. Cook seafood, flipping once, until pores and skin are crisp, 4-5 moments; transfer to a plate. Add five-spice powder and chiles; cook 1-2 moments. Add onion; prepare until somewhat caramelized, 8-10 moments. Add reserved spices, garlic, ginger, and 1 1/2 cups drinking water; boil. Add tomatoes; prepare until thickened, 8-10 minutes. Stir in seafood and the cilantro.

INDIAN SPICED CHICKPEA FLATBREAD {SOCCA}

Servings: 4

INGREDIENTS

- 2 cups chickpea or garbanzo bean flour
- 2 cups water
- 6 tablespoons + 2 teaspoons extra virgin olive oils divided
- 1 teaspoon ground coriander
- 1/2 teaspoon ground turmeric
- 1 teaspoon salt
- 1/4 - 1/4 teaspoon cayenne pepper
- 1 medium yellow onion chopped
- 2/3 cup diced tomatoes
- 2 garlic cloves minced
- 1/4 cup minced cilantro

DIRECTIONS

1. In a moderate bowl, whisk jointly the chickpea flour, water, 1 tablespoon plus 1 teaspoon essential olive oil, salt, ground coriander, and turmeric.
2. Cover with plastic material wrap and allow mixture rest at area temperature for at least 2 hours.
3. Preheat the broiler, with the rack set 7 to 8 in . from the element.
4. High temperature 1 teaspoon of essential olive oil in a sizable nonstick skillet place over medium-high heat.

5. Add the onion and prepare until needs to brown, about 2 minutes. Mix in the tomato and prepare for three minutes. Add the garlic and make for 30 seconds. Mix the vegetables into the chickpea flour batter.

6. Place a huge (10-in .) cast-iron skillet in the oven to preheat for five minutes.

7. Using an oven mitt or potholder, carefully take away the cast iron skillet from the oven. Pour in 1 tablespoon essential olive oil and swirl to coating the pan.

8. Pour in two of the batter and instantly swirl to coat underneath the pan.

9. Place beneath the broiler and make until the best and edges are beginning to blacken and blister, four to six 6 minutes.

10. Cautiously transfer the flatbread to a cutting board, cut into 8 wedges, garnish with cilantro and serve.

11. Repeat with the rest of the 1 tablespoon essential olive oil, butter, and cilantro.

MALIKA MASOOR DAL (RED LENTILS WITH GREEN MANGO)

Servings: 4

INGREDIENTS

- 1 cup masoor dal (split red lentils), rinsed, soaked 30 minutes, and drained
- 1/2 tbsp. ground turmeric
- 3 amchoor slices (dried, green mango)
- 1/2 piece 1 (1") ginger, peeled and mashed into a paste
- 1/2 cup garlic (3 mashed into a paste, 12 peeled)
- kosher salt, to taste
- 1 1/2 tbsp. ghee
- 1 chiles de árbol, chopped
- 1 1/2 tbsp. roughly chopped cilantro, for garnish

DIRECTIONS

1. Bring dal, turmeric, garlic paste, the anchor slices, ginger paste, salt, and 6 cups drinking water to a boil in a 6-qt. saucepan. Reduce heat to moderate; cook, covered somewhat, until dal is normally mushy, about 20 minutes. Utilizing a whisk, vigorously mix dal until even and creamy.

2. Melt ghee within an 8" skillet over medium-high heat. Make peeled garlic and the chiles until golden, 4-5 a few minutes, and pour over dal; garnish with cilantro.

INSTANT POT BUTTER CHICKEN

Servings: 10

INGREDIENTS

- 2 tablespoons vegetable oil
- 2 tablespoons butter
- 1 1/2 tablespoons freshly grated ginger
- 2/3 cup garlic, crushed and roughly chopped
- 2 large onions, diced
- 2 cans 1 (6-oz.) tomato paste
- 4 pounds . boneless skinless chicken thighs, cut into 1" pieces
- 2 tablespoons garam masala
- 2 teaspoons paprika
- 2 tablespoons granulated sugar
- 2 teaspoons ground cumin
- 1 teaspoon turmeric
- kosher salt
- freshly ground black pepper
- 1 1/2 cups heavy cream
- rice, for serving
- naan, for serving
- yogurt, for serving
- cilantro, for serving

DIRECTIONS

1. Preheat Quick Pot to Sauté environment. Once heated, add essential oil and butter after that add onion, ginger, and garlic. Allow sear until gently browned, three to four 4 mins. Add tomato paste and make, mixing continuously until it really is darkened in color, about three minutes. Add 1/2 cup water, poultry, and spices to the pot, and time of year with salt and pepper. Seal lid and arranged to Pressure Make on High for five minutes. Let pressure launch naturally for ten minutes and follow the manufacturer's guidelines for quick releasing staying steam. Stir in weighty cream and modify seasoning with salt and pepper. Serve with rice, naan, yogurt, and cilantro.

KASHMIRI HOT SAUCE

Servings: 10

INGREDIENTS

- 1 teaspoon fennel seeds
- 1/2 teaspoon black or brown mustard seeds
- 10 fresh red chiles (such as fresno)
- 1/4 cup distilled white vinegar

- 2 medium tomatoes, halved crosswise, seeds removed
- 2 teaspoons kashmiri chili powder or paprika
- 2 teaspoons kosher salt
- 1 teaspoon sugar
- a spice mill or mortar and pestle

DIRECTIONS

1. Toast fennel seeds and mustard seeds in a dried-out small saucepan over moderate heat, shaking pan frequently, until fragrant, about 45 mere seconds. Transfer to a plate and allow awesomely. Finely grind in a spice mill or with mortar and pestle. Transfer back again to pan.

2. Pulse tomato and chiles in a meals processor until the fine floor. Transfer to a saucepan with floor spices and blend in vinegar, chili powder, salt, and sugar. Bring to a simmer over moderate heat, stirring often; prepare until chiles are gentle and sauce is somewhat thickened, 5-7 a few minutes. Let cool.

3. Do Forward: Hot sauce could be made 1 week forward. Cover and chill.

INSTANT POT INDIAN BUTTER SHRIMP

Servings: 8

INGREDIENTS

- 1/2 cup plain whole-milk yogurt
- 1 1/2 tablespoons ground cumin
- 1 1/2 tablespoons garam masala
- 1 1/2 tablespoons lime juice
- 1 1/2 tablespoons sweet paprika
- 1 tablespoon kosher salt
- 2 teaspoons freshly grated ginger, use a microplane if you have one
- 2 garlic cloves, grated with a microplane or minced
- 4 pounds large shrimp, peeled and deveined
- 1/2 cup butter, divided
- 4 shallots, minced
- 4 garlic cloves, grated or minced
- 1 tablespoon grated fresh ginger
- 2 teaspoon crushed red pepper flakes
- 1/2 teaspoon kosher salt
- 2 (28-ounce) cans diced tomatoes, with juice
- 2 cups heavy cream
- 1 teaspoon finely grated limes zest

- cooked basmati rice
- chopped fresh cilantro

DIRECTIONS

1. In a moderate bowl, mix jointly yogurt, cumin, paprika, garam masala, lime juice, salt, ginger, and garlic to create a marinade. Mix in shrimp. Refrigerate for a quarter-hour to at least one 1 hour.
2. While shrimp is marinating, prepare the sauce. Convert Quick Pot to "saute" and add 2 tablespoons butter.
3. Once the butter has melted, combine shallots and a pinch of salt. Make until golden brown, four to six 6 minutes.
4. Mix in garlic, ginger, crimson pepper flakes, and 1/4 teaspoon salt and cook another one to two 2 minutes.
5. Mix in tomatoes and their juice, large cream, and another pinch of salt. Bring the mix to a boil. After that cover and place on ruthless for 8 a few minutes. Make certain valve is considered "sealing". Discharge the pressure manually. When the pin drops, take away the lid.
6. Turn on the "saute" setting and simmer the sauce to thicken about 4 to 7 a few minutes.
7. Mix in the shrimp and marinade, the rest of the 2 tablespoons butter, and the lime zest and make 2 to five minutes, or until shrimp are pink, being careful never to overcook. They will continue steadily to make in the sauce once you take them off from the moment Pot.
8. Serve with rice and cilantro.

QUICK CHICKEN CURRY

Serves: 4-6 **- Preparation Time:** 5 minutes **- Cooking time:** 15-20 minutes

INGREDIENTS

- 2-3 pounds cooked chicken, poached or roasted
- 1 ½ tablespoons mustard or vegetable oil
- 1 small onion, thinly sliced
- 1 teaspoon ginger, grated
- 3 cloves garlic, minced
- 1 tablespoon curry powder
- ½-1 teaspoon red chili flakes
- 1 medium tomato, diced
- ½ cup yogurt
- 1 (14-ounce) can coconut milk
- 1-2 pieces bay leaf
- ½ teaspoon salt, or to taste
- ¼ teaspoon black pepper

- ½ teaspoon sugar (optional)
- ¼ cup fresh cilantro leaves, roughly chopped
- 1 cup white rice

DIRECTIONS

1. shred the pre-cooked chicken, or cut it into bite-sized pieces.
2. heat the oil in a frying pan or wok over medium-high heat and sauté the onions and ginger until fragrant and the onion is tender (about 5-8 minutes).
3. add garlic and sauté about a minute longer until fragrant.
4. add the chicken and stir-fry. for roast chicken pieces, heat through. if you're using poached chicken, cook until slightly browned.
5. add the curry powder, chili flakes and tomato. stir-fry for about 3 minutes, or until the tomatoes are slightly mushy.
6. reduce the heat to medium-low and add yogurt, coconut milk, bay leaves, black pepper, salt, and sugar (optional). stir and simmer until thickened, about 3-5 minutes.
7. adjust the seasoning and spices, if desired.
8. remove from the heat, sprinkle with cilantro, and serve with rice or naan.

CHICKEN MADRAS

Serves: 4 - **Preparation Time:** 30 minutes - **Cooking time:** 30 minutes to 1 hour

INGREDIENTS

- 4 boneless skinless chicken breasts or thighs, cut into bite-sized pieces

For marinade:

- 1 ½ tablespoons freshly squeezed lemon juice
- 1 teaspoon garam masala
- Salt, to taste

For sauce:

- 2 tablespoons ghee or vegetable oil
- 1 large onion, finely chopped
- 3-5 tablespoons Madras curry paste
- 1 (16-ounce) can chopped tomatoes
- ½ cup desiccated coconut

For garnish:

- ¼ cup fresh cilantro, chopped

DIRECTIONS

1. combine the ingredients for the marinade and toss in the chicken pieces. set aside.
2. heat the oil in a karahi/wok, or frying pan. sauté the onion until it is almost golden in color (5-8

minutes).

3. add the chicken and cook for 5 minutes, stirring constantly.

4. add the madras paste and stir to distribute the flavor, than cook for 2 more minutes.

5. add the tomato and coconut, cover, and let it simmer for 20 minutes. the chicken should be cooked through.

6. add more salt or madras paste, if desired.

7. garnish with cilantro and serve with rice or naan.

BUTTER CHICKEN (MURGH MAKHAN)

Serves: 6 - **Preparation Time:** 15 minutes - **Cooking time:** 45 minutes

INGREDIENTS

- 1 cup butter, divided
- 1 onion, minced
- 1 tablespoon minced garlic
- 1 ½ pounds boneless skinless chicken breast, cut into bite-sized chunks
- 2 tablespoons vegetable oil
- 2 tablespoons tandoori masala
- 1 (15-ounce) can tomato sauce
- 3 cups heavy cream
- 2 teaspoons salt
- 1 teaspoon cayenne pepper
- 1 teaspoon garam masala

DIRECTIONS

1. preheat the oven to 375°f.

2. take about 2 tablespoons of the butter and melt it in a karahi (or any skillet) over medium heat.

3. add the onion and garlic and cook for 15 minutes, stirring occasionally, or until the onion becomes dark brown in color.

4. in a bowl, combine the chicken with the oil and toss to coat. add the tandoori masala and mix well.

5. arrange the chicken pieces in one layer on a baking sheet.

6. bake for about 12 minutes, or until the chicken is thoroughly cooked.

7. in another pan, melt the rest of the butter over medium-high heat.

8. stir in the tomato sauce, cream, salt, cayenne, and garam masala.

9. reduce the heat to medium low and simmer for 30 minutes.

10. add the caramelized onion and the baked chicken, and simmer for 5 minutes.

GOAN FISH CURRY

Serves: 4-6 **- Preparation Time:** 15 minutes **- Cooking time:** 20-30 minutes

INGREDIENTS

- 2 tablespoons vegetable oil
- 1 large onion, finely chopped
- 4 large cloves fresh garlic, minced
- 1 cup water
- 1 teaspoon salt, or to taste
- 1 cup coconut milk
- 2-3 tablespoons tamarind paste
- 1 ½ pounds fish fillets, 1 inch thick, cut into 2-inch pieces
- ¼ cup finely chopped fresh cilantro, including soft stems

For spice mix:

- 3 dried red chili peppers, broken into pieces
- 1 teaspoon coriander seeds
- 1 teaspoon cumin seeds
- ¼ teaspoon ground turmeric

DIRECTIONS

1. grind together the red chili peppers, coriander, cumin, and turmeric in a small spice grinder. set aside.
2. heat the oil in a large nonstick wok or saucepan over medium-high heat and stir-fry the onion for 5 minutes or until golden.
3. add the garlic and stir 1 minute, then stir in the spice mixture and cook 2 minutes more.
4. pour in the water and coconut milk. bring to a boil, stirring constantly. reduce the heat and simmer for 5 minutes.
5. add the tamarind paste and salt. stir well.
6. add the fish and continue simmering for 10-15 minutes, or until the fish is opaque and easy to flake with a fork.
7. sprinkle with cilantro and serve.

FISH SKEWERS (FISH TANDOORI TIKKA)

Serves: 4 **- Preparation Time:** 10 minutes plus 8 hours and 10 minutes marinating time **- Cooking time:** 15 minutes

INGREDIENTS

- 1 ½ pounds fish fillets, cut into 1 ½-inch cubes

For first marinade:

- Salt, to taste
- ⅛ teaspoon red chili powder
- 4 tablespoons freshly squeezed lemon juice

For second marinade:

- 1 cup yogurt
- ½ teaspoon garam masala
- ¼ teaspoon red chili powder
- ¼ teaspoon cumin powder
- ¼ teaspoon pepper powder
- 2 cloves garlic, minced
- 1 teaspoon ginger, minced

For garnish:

- Pinch of chaat masala
- Lemon wedges

DIRECTIONS

1. wipe the fish with paper towels to dry.
2. gently rub the ingredients for the first marinade all over the fish. cover, and refrigerate for 10 minutes.
3. in a bowl, combine ingredients for second marinade.
4. gently massage the mixture onto the fish and let it marinate for 6-8 hours.
5. skewer the fish pieces and grill for about 7-8 minutes on each side.
6. sprinkle with chaat masala and serve with wedges of lemon.

MIXED SEAFOOD CURRY

Serves: 6 - **Preparation Time:** 20 minutes - **Cooking time:** 15 minutes

INGREDIENTS

- 2 tablespoons vegetable oil
- 1 medium onion, halved and sliced
- 1 tablespoon ginger, minced
- 1 tablespoon garlic, minced
- 2-3 pieces green chili
- ½ teaspoon red chili powder (optional)
- ½ teaspoon turmeric powder
- 1 (14-ounce) can light coconut milk
- 3 tablespoons lime juice

- 1 tablespoons curry powder, or according to taste
- 1 tablespoon brown sugar
- 12 medium shrimp, peeled (tails left on) and deveined
- 12 sea scallops, halved
- 2 tablespoons chopped cilantro
- Salt to taste

DIRECTIONS

1. heat oil in a karahi/kadai or wok over medium-high heat.
2. sauté the onion until tender, about 2-3 minutes.
3. stir in the ginger, garlic, and green chili, and sauté until fragrant, about 1 minute.
4. add red chili powder (optional), turmeric, coconut milk, lime juice, curry powder, and brown sugar. bring to a simmer and cook for 5 minutes.
5. add the shrimp, scallops, cilantro, and salt, and cook until the shrimps and scallops become opaque, about 5 minutes.
6. adjust the flavor with more salt and spices if needed.

www.ingramcontent.com/pod-product-compliance
Lightning Source LLC
Chambersburg PA
CBHW060605120726
48002CB00010B/2832